Easy Be

Diana Beaver is a Member of the Association of NLP,
a Member of The Institute of Linguists and
a Member of The International Association of Master Trainers.
She works as a consultant, coach and trainer of NLP in any area that grabs
her interest.

By the same author

Lazy Learning: Making the Most of the Brains You Were Born With

(Element Books)

For my friend Robert
With my love as always
Diana
22 ix.97

Easy Being

MAKING LIFE AS SIMPLE AND AS MUCH FUN AS POSSIBLE

Diana Beaver

So That he can discover how much easier being can be.

USEFUL BOOK COMPANY

Published in Great Britain in 1997 by
The Useful Book Company
P O Box 48, Cirencester, GL7 5YE
in association with the Anglo-American Book Company

Design and graphics by AuthorDocs, Swindon, Wiltshire
Photographs by Roger Phillips
Cover:
Design: Brian Curd
Photographs: Roger Phillips
Advisors: Matthew Curd & Richard Ayliffe

Printed and bound in Great Britain by
Redwood Books, Trowbridge, Wiltshire

British Library Cataloguing in Publication Data
A catalogue record for this book is available from the British Library
ISBN 0 9531003 0 8

Dedication

This book is for my friend, teacher and mentor, Judith DeLozier,
who taught me that life is a dance.
Judy is all about being.
Judy just is.

And in memory of that kindliest of wolves,
the late Todd Epstein,
who contributed more to this than he, or I, will ever know.

It is also - as always - for my menfolk,
Philip, Mark and Hugo,
with my love.

Contents

Acknowledgements

As always, I would like to thank all the friends, teachers and mentors that I have been lucky enough to work with:

Richard Bandler
Charlotte Bretto
Judith DeLozier
Robert Dilts
the late Todd Epstein
Lara Ewing
the late David Gaster
Stephen Gilligan
John Grinder
Ian McDermott
Joseph O'Connor
Julian Russell
Titos Sompa

and all my students, clients and colleagues, from whom I have learned so much.

As usual, my thanks to all the friends and colleagues who have given me permission to plunder their work. I hope I have given credit where credit is due and, if not, that I will be forgiven.

The easy bit is writing the book; it's the last bit that's tricky. Getting *Lazy Learning* ready for publication was a nightmare; *Easy Being* was a breeze - thanks to the brilliant UBC support team who did all the difficult bits: Peter Gilbert for his sensitive copy editing, and Margaret for the good food; Brian Curd of AuthorDocs, for the design, and the ease with which he was prepared to take on anything; Bill Norris of Central Books for his enthusiasm and good ideas; David Bowman of Anglo-American Books for support and more good ideas - and also Glenys and Martin Roberts of AA Books, who have supported everything I've done; everyone at Redwood Books - particularly for the quality of their welcome - and Simon Povey for finding Peter; Belinda Boyd of Pulse Communications, who is good at her job because she is good at being who she is; Peter Finch of the Oriel Bookshop in Cardiff for all the practical advice, which made everything so simple; Mark Hartery who does the sums, and supports everything I do, and as always my husband Philip for the uncountable hours spent getting the computer to do what I needed it to do.

All these people provided what I needed as though it was the easiest thing in the world and, above all, amused and entertained me along the way.

SECRET

The Ministry of Anti-Fun
Whitehall
London SW1

MEMORANDUM
To: All Heads of Department
From: The Minister

It has been brought to my attention that there are still large areas of life where people are *enjoying themselves.*

There are four factors in dealing with a problem of this magnitude. All Departments should arrange to create (via the media) the following conditions, throughout this country.

1. Blame

Start by blaming the Americans. In particular a man called Richard Bandler who openly professes that the main problem with this world is that people take themselves too seriously. Bandler comes from New Jersey - a state with a well-known attitude problem (NB: do not allow yourselves to be drawn into discussions about his academic qualifications, etc). You can also mention that he is Jewish - more scope for blame. Then there is a man called John Grinder: he is also dangerous, but keeps a lower profile (NB Grinder is of Irish descent). As above, avoid discussions on academic qualifications. These two men are highly undesirable and strenuous efforts should be made to prevent them, and shipments of their books, from coming into this country.

Other undesirable foreigners: Judith DeLozier masquerades as a cow-girl from Oklahoma, whereas our intelligence shows that she is, in fact, of Basque origin; Robert Dilts is of Irish origin, and worked with the late Todd Epstein (another Jew from New Jersey); and Stephen Gilligan: another Irishman. In this country, Diana Beaver masquerades as a respectable Englishwoman, whereas our intelligence shows that she is also Irish.

People can draw their own conclusions about the ancestry of these undesirables, and the fact that all the Americans now live in California, which has a reputation for producing weirdos.

The above-mentioned spread sedition by maintaining that *individuals are important*; that they matter; that *they have the right and the ability to be happy and fulfilled*; and that *they can take charge of their own lives*.

2. Guilt

Happiness, joy, fulfilment, success, etc, must of necessity be:

- Immoral
- At someone else's expense
- Undeserved
- Greedy
- Selfish
- Dishonest
- Not cricket

3. Polarisation

It must be made quite clear to the people of this country, via the media, that things are either good or bad (in this case bad); there can be no middle ground. The following should be used to further this campaign:

- Pundits who know best and take a high moral tone
- Churchmen who know that God and Fun cannot go together
- Politicians who need publicity

NB: It is more effective to rubbish the people than to rubbish their policies. They are foreign; they are strangers; they are different and thus dangerous.

4. Jealousy

1. Anyone who is happier, more fulfilled, more successful or richer than anyone else must necessarily be doing something wrong. As must anyone who finds life easy and enjoyable.

2. If the man in the street cannot have something, then no one else has a right to it either. For example, the man in the street has not got a Royal Yacht; there is therefore no reason why Her Majesty the Queen should have one.

3. Following from 2 above, banning other people's fun gets votes.

We really cannot have the people of this country enjoying themselves; before we know where we are, they will be thinking for themselves, and that would never do.

Any further suggestions for combating this serious problem would therefore be most welcome.

N B Ighmer-Payne

Introduction

Does your life ever seem to be more complicated than it needs to be?
Would your life be perfect if it were not for other people?
Would you like to have more time to enjoy your self?
Would you like to have more fun?

If you enjoy living a life which is complicated and difficult, then this is not the book for you; if, on the other hand, you would like life to be simpler, so that you could have more time, be more effective, more productive, and more fulfilled - as well as having much more fun at home, at work and at play - then read on.

Another question: *Are you a human being, or are you a robot?* Robots are both logical and predictable - humans are not. This book explores the structure of how and why we behave in the ways that we do. It also explores how and why we give ourselves such a hard time; and what we can do to change things - so that we can give ourselves the best, in order to be our best.

Lazy Learning introduced NLP (Neuro-Linguistic Programming) as a way of rediscovering the natural learning abilities we were all born with. The purpose of *Easy Being* is to take the curious reader back a step or two; to the beliefs and presuppositions behind NLP; in other words, to the thinking which created this fascinating field of apparently endless possibilities.

Our reactions to life, the universe and everything depend largely upon our beliefs and presuppositions; for example: on the subject of other people - if we walk into a room full of strangers in the belief that they are going to tear us limb from limb (which is physically possible) we are unlikely to enjoy the experience; if, on the other hand, we believe that these people are going to welcome us and enjoy our company, then we are going to enjoy ourselves. Or, if we think about machines, some adults believe that any form of modern technology is beyond them, and so the thought of making life easier by using a computer is instantly dismissed; whereas children, who have never been troubled with this belief, can master computers in next to no time.

The rapid growth of NLP in almost every field is simply because it works. It is often considered to be just a series of powerful, fast and effective techniques, which can be used to create change, for example:

The Phobia Cure

The Spelling Strategy

The Walt Disney Strategy for Creativity

It is very exciting when one minute there is a phobia, and the next minute it is gone. It is amazing to discover that you could have been an excellent speller all your life, if you had only known how to use your learning equipment in the appropriate way for spelling. It is fascinating to become deeply aware of how creative you have always been without noticing it, and to experience how this creativity grows and develops all the time, once you are aware of what you do and how you do it.

This is all great stuff and very useful; it could be described as the NLP demonstration pack - a series of instant selling points: show that it works, and the punters will buy. And maybe we present it like this because we feel that no down-to-earth, practical person will be attracted by the thought that the success of any NLP 'technique' is probably due to the profound connection between the people who are working together, rather than the technique itself.

The early learning process of NLP can be like a series of party tricks: look what I can do! Aren't I clever! And there is a lot to be said for this: would-be Practitioners discover that they can create changes for themselves and other people that they would never have believed possible, and this gives them the confidence to grow and to develop with everything that they learn.

But, of course, like anything else, the techniques are simply by-products of the thinking behind them - in the same way that classical design is a by-product of a deeply ingrained sense of geometry; or that communication skills are a by-product of a deeply held belief that people are fascinating.

Easy Being will help you to decide whether or not you really want an easy life - some people would be miserable without their dramas: they stimulate them and give them lots to talk about. For example, a friend telephoned me with a catalogue of woes, and capped it by saying: 'and, of course, I'm crippled with arthritis now!' While she was evidently enjoying dumping all her rubbish on me, I was getting extremely bored, and a thought came to me: 'What would happen', I asked, 'if you let go of the arthritis?'

'I dread to think!' came the immediate reply. What a fascinating answer! Maybe she felt that, if she did not have the stiffness of the arthritis to hold her together, she would fall apart - who knows?

Easy Being will enable you to try on our presuppositions for size, so that you can discover what would happen if they became yours as well; so that you can experiment with how they would change your reactions to life, the universe and everything, and allow you to achieve mastery in whatever field you choose.

If you decide that simplicity and fun are what you want, then these presuppositions will provide you with a solid base from which to experiment further with enjoying your self and creating a world which you will enjoy living in.

Explore the ideas; try the experiments; play the games; and have fun!

Part I:
On Giving Ourselves a Hard Time

If you have decided that you want your life to be simpler and more fun, the first thing we need to ask is, what is stopping it from being simple and fun in the first place?

- Is it events?
- Is it other people?
- Is it you?
- Or is it something completely different?

Take a moment to think about this question. You might like to put your thoughts down on paper, and add to them as ideas come to you.

Ask other people, and see what they come up with. Because we are all so different, the answers you will get will be very varied; some of them may make complete sense to you while others may seem completely weird.

One of the main reasons for not enjoying life to the full is that we all give ourselves a hard time. Most of us treat ourselves worse than we treat our worst enemies; we go around according other people tremendous respect, while respect for ourselves is sorely lacking. By respect, I mean things like: giving ourselves the time and space to sort ourselves out; paying attention to our needs; appreciating our good points and our achievements - and all the other ways we show respect to other people.

(You will be able to think of dozens of other ways in which you treat yourself worse than you treat other people. Find a pencil and paper, and write them down. Be honest: no one else is going to see your list. And, as time goes by, you will become more and more aware of how you are abusing your own human rights; add these to your list, and make a mental note that you owe me £50 every time you re-offend.)

Most of this maltreatment of ourselves happens because we simply do not bother to take the time and the trouble to think about what we are and are not doing.

Starting to Think More Usefully

Hamlet said: '*There is nothing either good or bad, but thinking makes it so*' - there wasn't much about human nature that Shakespeare missed.

Things just are. It is the way we think about them which decides what effect they are going to have upon us. For example, if we are stuck in a traffic jam, we have a choice of working ourselves up into a frenzy, or of relaxing and waiting to see what happens, or of doing something completely different: however we are going to react, the choice is ours - no one else can make it for us.

So how can NLP help us to make some useful changes to the way that we think? We could start with some thoughts about what NLP is.

The name Neuro-Linguistic Programming is guaranteed to glaze the eyes of any polite enquirer; and NLP-ers like an easy life, so probably the only time we give this endlessly fascinating field its full title is when we are explaining to the curious the basics of this combination of art and techniques - to demonstrate how people can use it to create a change they want, in any area that they choose.

Neuro: is about our neurology; about the connections between all parts of the body; about the connections between our thoughts and our bodies; about how the brain affects the body and how the body affects the brain.

Try an experiment:

1. Spend a few moments thinking about someone you like (Person A) - someone whom you really enjoy being with - and experience what goes on inside you as you conjure up images of that person, maybe seeing a certain look on their face, hearing the sound of their voice, and feeling whatever you feel when you are with them.

2. Think about someone you do not react well to (Person B) - someone you would avoid being with, if you possibly could - and notice what goes on inside you this time. Your internal experience will be quite different from what it was when you were thinking about Person A. For example, what differences do you notice in the feelings in your stomach as you think about each one?

3. You could then explore the differences further by switching your thoughts backwards and forwards from one person to the other, and noticing the differences in the pictures in your mind's eye, the sounds in your mind's ear and the rest of your feelings - for example: your breathing, your heart rate, the amount of saliva in your mouth.

4. Spend some time thinking about a favourite moment with Person A: this will settle you back into a good internal state.

Another version of this exercise is to think about something you love doing: maybe a favourite hobby; and then think about something you hate doing: maybe your accounts. Then compare and contrast what goes on inside you in the same way that you did with A and B. Once again, if you spend time doing this, you will find that your internal reactions are completely different.

As you will have discovered, it requires no more than a thought to change the feelings in your body. Even to this day, the thought of the arrival of my school report brings a dryness to my throat and a heavy feeling to my stomach: my school report was generally the trigger for severe disapproval, lengthy discussions of my faults and a bad atmosphere which could be reproduced at any moment until the end of the holidays.

Now try an experiment to demonstrate how the body affects the brain:

Think of something that seriously depresses you and try to maintain that depressed feeling while walking about briskly, looking up at the sky, or the tree tops or, if you are indoors, where the wall meets the ceiling - whatever is high enough in your field of vision to keep your eyes raised; you will find that it is impossible to retain all those uncomfortable thoughts when your eyes are raised.

The patent Beaver remedy for depression is to take the sufferer kite-flying, without telling them why; so that they can allow themselves the time and freedom to let go of the depressed feelings, while watching the antics of the kite in the air.

Linguistic: is about how the language we use expresses, from a deep, subconscious level, what is going on inside us. We process information in different ways: some of us prefer to do it through our eyes, some of us

through our ears, and some of us through our feelings. If you hear someone's conversation interspersed with visual language like:

- *Look*!
- I *see* what you mean
- I can't *see* the point
- Let me *see*
- Let's get this *clear*
- From my point of *view*

you will know that they are processing their thoughts through internal pictures.

If you hear auditory language, like:

- *Listen*!
- That *rings* a bell
- That *sounds* right
- Something *tells* me
- It's *music* to my ears
- We don't *speak* the same language

you will realise that they are processing through sounds.

And if the language is all about feelings:

- He's a *pain* in the neck
- I can't *grasp* what you're saying
- It was very *touching*
- *Hold* on!
- I can't *bear* it
- It was heart-*warming*

this person is processing through their body.

The other two senses, taste and smell, often demonstrate a very basic
awareness.

- It *smells* fishy
- I *smell* a rat
- It *stinks*
- He's in bad *odour*
- It was a *bitter* experience
- It leaves a nasty *taste* in your mouth
- Sugaring the *pill*
- A joke in extremely poor *taste*

You can test this out by trying another experiment:

Get a friend to spend some time telling you about his or her latest passion, and listen to the language that he or she uses to describe it. You will discover just how what you are hearing is being processed. The information may be coming from internal pictures, from sounds, from feelings, or from any combination of these, with some tastes and smells thrown in.

And, if you are on your own:

Listen to the language that people use when they are talking on the radio, or television - for example a chat show, or an interview - and discover how they have organised their thoughts.

The interesting thing about all this is that, if we change our language, we change our thinking.

We can give ourselves a seriously hard time by berating ourselves with words like 'should' and 'ought to'. Try deleting these bullying words from your vocabulary, and discover how your relationship with yourself becomes much more comfortable. How do you respond to being told that you should/ought to do something by somebody else? The American Educationalist, Barbara Meister Vitale, expresses our natural reaction succinctly, by saying: 'Don't "should" on me!'.

Programming: refers to the automatic programs that we run in our heads to simplify life - they are the short cuts that our brain has created to save going through repetitive thought processes. For example, when the traffic lights turn red, we could react by running through a lengthy list of possible interpretations of this phenomenon, followed by another list of things we might do about it, and then spend time thinking how to do what we have decided to do; however, our brains are far too efficient to waste all this time and effort, so they create an automatic, streamlined labour/time-saving program:

1. See a red light
2. Brake

The same thing happens when someone holds out their right hand to us: we shake it; or when someone smiles at us: we smile back. We do not stop to wonder why they are doing what they are doing, we just react.

Most of our programs are very useful, but some may be out of date: we may still panic at the mention of maths because the teacher, or the person we sat next to in class, was a bully. That panic was quite proper at the time - it was to get us out of trouble; but that bully has long since disappeared out of our lives so the program can do the same, and be replaced by whatever we choose as being more appropriate reactions for who we are now.

Phobias come into the same category: the initial reaction got us out of trouble, and we gave ourselves such a fright that the brain decided that, for safety's sake, this reaction was guaranteed to keep us alive. Once the brain becomes aware of all the other available choices of behaviour, it will obligingly update the program and give us a series of choices in how to react.

Choices are what we need: if we once had a phobia of snakes and now, phobia-free, we meet a real live cobra who is demonstrating that he wants us off his patch, this is the moment for us to demonstrate - at speed - our respect for another creature's territorial rights, rather than our new-found interest in the beauty of snakes, which necessitates closer inspection; the choice of closer inspection of poisonous snakes is only appropriate for full colour pictures of dangerous snakes in books and magazines, or for snakes behind reinforced glass.

The important thing to remember about your brain is that it is yours, and works exclusively for you and in your best interests; and that it does the very best that it possibly can with the information available to it at the time. Your brain is there to protect you; and protect you it will, to the best of its ability: it just needs to know what you want, so that it can do its job most effectively.

* * * * *

In the early 1970s Dr Richard Bandler, PhD, was a student at the University of California in Santa Cruz. Richard was a mathematician, physicist and computer wizard (in other words he had a respectable, logical brain) and he was passionately interested in therapy. Dr John Grinder, PhD, Professor of Linguistics at the UCSC (despite having been told when younger that he would never master a foreign language), used to go along to Richard's therapy seminars. These two joined forces in search of some answers, for example: *what was the difference that made the difference between therapists who were effective and those who were not?* What was special about what the effective ones said, what they did and what they believed, when they were working with clients?

They discovered that the magic trick was simply to join your client in his or her model of the world, so that you can experience for yourself what is going on there, and then lead them out of it and into a more useful place. In order to do this, the successful therapists spoke the same language as their clients: in other words, when a client said he felt *heavy and down*, the successful therapist would reply in the language of feelings (known in the trade as kinaesthetic - if you remember that the kinema/cinema shows *moving* pictures, 'kinaesthetic' is an easy piece of jargon). The less effective therapists might be telling the client to *look at the problem, and get it into perspective* - visual language that meant nothing to someone who felt trapped in their feelings. The effective therapists were also matching or mirroring their clients' body posture and movements, and matching their breathing: establishing an unconscious bond, so that their clients felt connected and valued. And then, once this bond was safely established, they could lead their clients into a more useful state for the change that they wanted.

Having created a model of the structure of successful therapy that worked, they then went on to model the structure of excellence in other fields like selling, marksmanship, acting, healing, and so on. They became modellers of excellence, searching for 'the difference that makes the difference' (a phrase borrowed from their friend and neighbour, the English anthropologist, Gregory Bateson, who was one of the great thinkers of our time); in other words, rather than take on the entire persona of Diego Maradona in order to become a brilliant footballer, all we need to do is to discover the difference that makes the difference - it may be a belief that Maradona holds, it may be a strategy that he uses that makes him a star on the football field. Whatever it is, once we know, we can use it.

So how did something so simple get such a complicated name? Richard tells the story about how he was stopped by the police in California and asked what his occupation was. Realising that he had no label for what he did, he glanced round the car in search of inspiration, and saw a book on Neurology, a book on Linguistics and a book on Computer Programming.

'I am a Neuro-Linguistic Programmer', he announced; and the policeman was apparently most impressed.

My introduction to NLP was a book called '*Frogs into Princes*' by Richard and John - with a title like that, it had to be good; so I read it, and it blew my mind. Here were these two apparent lunatics proving to me all those things that I had always known, but which were too simple for the rest of the world to believe in. And, what was more, they made the point that what they were telling me was not necessarily the truth - it was just a useful way of thinking and being: a way that worked for them.

NLP-ers take themselves with several large pinches of salt. We look for the simplest, easiest most fun ways of achieving our outcomes - always aware that what works for one person may not work for the next: the techniques that we use are just techniques and may be created on the spur of the moment. And the fun of our work is that everyone is different, so we are learning all the time. Everything that we do is based upon a series of presuppositions; and, in case, like me, you are immediately put off by words of more than three syllables, let's think for a moment about what 'presupposition' means:

- '*What is your next car going to be?*' presupposes that you already have a car - otherwise, I would not have used the word 'next'.
- '*Would you like a drink, before you order?*' presupposes that you are going to order something.
- '*Would you like a story before you go to bed?*' - presupposes that the child is going to go to bed, rather than stay up for hours.
- '*We'll have tea when you get back from your walk*' presupposes that you are going for a walk.

In other words, each one of these statements or questions is based upon another thought that lies behind it - something that we have supposed in advance. And NLP-ers suppose in advance that certain things are so: we do not maintain that these presuppositions are true, they just fit comfortably with who we are and what we are doing on the planet; and we also find that they are a simple, powerful, flexible basis from which to live and work, because they give people choices, and allow them to take responsibility for themselves.

The Map is not the Territory

We use this metaphor to illustrate that 'reality', as such, cannot exist: because we are all different; and, because we all represent reality in the way that we experience it for ourselves, your version of reality will not necessarily correspond with mine.

The world out there is so enormous and complex that we cannot get it all inside our heads and so, in order to simplify things, we code and file information in our brains so that we can retrieve it later. As we were not born with brain handbooks, we have to work out how to do this as we go along, and we devise all sorts of weird and wonderful strategies for recording what goes on in our lives. The most interesting thing about all this is that, because there are no hard and fast rules, there are a million and one ways that people do it. Some of us do most of our coding and filing in pictures, some of us do it through sounds, some of us do it through our feelings; and some of us use combinations of two or all three systems. There are also tastes and smells which we can add to our retrieval arrangements. And, on top of all this, we all file our information in different places in our brains.

'The Map is not the Territory' illustrates the fact that everybody processes 'reality' in their own way. If I ask you to think of maths lessons at school, the way that you represent this idea to yourself will vary according to the experiences that you had at the time. If you loved maths, you may get a lovely warm glow inside and see bright, clear pictures in your mind's eye; if you hated maths, your internal pictures may be huge and dark (making you feel small), there may be a nasty feeling in the pit of your stomach, and you may have a voice in your mind's ear saying that you can't do/don't understand maths; alternatively, whatever happens inside you at the mention of the word 'maths' may be completely different.

Whatever you are experiencing, it is not reality: you are not in a maths class now, you are simply reading this book and responding to one of my suggestions.

Here is an experiment for the benefit of those who may still feel stuck in a maths class:

Think of something that you absolutely love doing: it could be anything from sport to painting; and enjoy experiencing what goes on inside you, for a bit, so that you can bring yourself back into a good state.

NB. You can do this last bit any time you need to cheer yourself up.

Our version of reality also depends on our perspective: for example, try getting someone to drive you along a fast road, parallel to the take-off/landing path of an airport: if you are going in the opposite direction to the aircraft, you will notice the extraordinary speed and angle at which they gain height - quite unlike what you experience when you are inside an aeroplane; you will also notice how descending aircraft seem to hang, almost motionless in the air. When you turn round and drive in the same direction as the aircraft, they will seem to behave quite differently.

Alternatively, to save a journey to an airport, try watching the moon, dancing along beside you through the clouds, as you are being driven along in a car; and notice how, when the car stops, the moon stops dancing and hangs, still and beautiful, in the sky.

Everything that you observe in these two experiments is reality to you, at the time; it is the truth, according to the information that you have available to you.

'If we think about the metaphor of a map, we will realise that it is a representation of an area of land which has been created to help people to find their way from A to B. There are different kinds of maps to meet different needs: if I am looking for somewhere nice to walk my dog, I will need an Ordnance Survey Map which marks public footpaths; if I want to work out how long it will take me to drive from London to Glasgow, I will need an overall map of Britain, with the motorway distances marked on it. A map is a two-dimensional miniaturised version of the territory: it has its own coding system for contours, for height above sea level, for different grades of roads, and so on. A map that was the territory would, for a start, have to be the same size and shape as the territory, which would destroy the point of a map as a useful, handy, simple reference.

The easy-to-interpret map of the London Underground has been distorted into rectangles which bear little relation to the actual shape of the rail connections. There is even a story of a Gurkha soldier, imprisoned far from his native Nepal, who escaped and found his way to friendly territory using a map of the London Underground, in the belief that it represented the territory he had to cross.

Your Ways are Your Ways - and My Ways are Mine

We all have our own models of reality. The way you perceive the world may have no connection with the way that I perceive it. And this is where the fun comes in.

As you discovered earlier, it is easy to know which system people are using to represent their reality by listening to their words and expressions:

- I want to put you in the picture
- Let's look at this from a different angle
- I see

show us that the person is in visual mode.

If we hear phrases like:

- It gives me a buzz
- That doesn't ring true
- We had a harmonious discussion

it sounds as though the person is in auditory mode.

While expressions like:

- My gut reaction is......
- I feel it in my bones
- I'm comfortable with that idea

give us the impression that the person is processing information through his or her body.

Most people process mainly through these three channels, which are reinforced by taste and smell. However, a friend of mine describes everything that I call 'beautiful' as 'yummy': I am primarily visual, and he is seriously into taste. Ask someone what something smells like, or to imagine they can smell lilac or newly-cut grass, and their nostrils will flare.

We can also tell which mode people are in by looking at their physiology - the way they hold themselves - and by the way they are breathing.

Recognising visual mode

When people are processing in pictures, you will see that their eyes flash up
to search for an answer; to look in the file where they keep their internal pictures. With most right-handed people remembered pictures will generally
be filed up, and to the left; whereas their constructed, that is to say imagined,
pictures will be filed up and to the right. Watch people talking and you will
discover where they keep their internal pictures; or test the theory out by
asking them questions like:

- What was I wearing last time you saw me?
- What colour are so-and-so's eyes?
- How to you spell 'excellent'?

and their eyes will flash up to the file where they keep remembered images.
If their eyes do not move, and yet they give you the right answer, your questions are too easy: ask them something more difficult so that they will have
to search harder for the information. These eye movements happen very
fast, so have the question in your head, so that you can see the immediate
response.

Some people may tell you firmly that they never make internal pictures,
in which case, you can wonder (out loud) how they recognise people: if you
and I had never met, and you had never seen a picture of me, I could introduce myself as Jane Jones and you would be none the wiser; whereas, if you
knew what I looked like (in other words, you had an internal picture of me),
you would compare what you saw with your internal picture and conclude
either that I was masquerading as somebody else, or that Jane Jones was
Diana Beaver's double.

In order to discover where people construct images in their mind's eye,
ask them to imagine something they have never seen before, for example:

- What would a penguin orchestra look like?
- What would a cat look like in purple pyjamas?
- What would racing greyhounds look like if they were ridden by
  monkeys?

People got wildly excited about the discovery of eye movements, and
thought that they were the be-all and end-all of NLP, to the extent that somebody walked out of a seminar that John Grinder was giving in Belgium saying, disgustedly: 'This isn't NLP, there's nothing about eye movements'.

They are fascinating and, as you will discover, they form just a tiny part of an enormous and even more fascinating field.

Apart from language, which we have already talked about, there are other ways of discovering what mode people are in. A person in visual mode will probably be holding themselves upright, while breathing quite fast into the upper chest and talking fast in a highish pitched voice (which may get higher as excitement rises); there may also be gestures at eye level, or above. If you listen to the architect, Sir Richard Rogers, (creator of the Centre Pompidou in Paris, among other things and, in my view, one of the most exciting architects of our time), you will discover that, the more he warms to his subject, the faster he speaks; architects are visionaries, and among the band of people who are paid to hallucinate things that are not there. (Incidentally, for anyone worrying about their children's learning abilities, Sir Richard had dyslexia or, as he puts it: 'It wasn't called dyslexia in my day, it was called laziness'.)

If you enjoy watching people in public places, you will notice that they walk in different ways; people whose feet are parallel as they walk are probably in visual mode. Watch the way that people walk up stairs: how much of their feet do they put on each step? Visual people will probably use the balls of their feet as leverage.

An easy way to remember all this is that visual mode seems to be 'up'; the eye movements, the physiology, the voice and the breathing; I always imagine that visual people are permanently trying to keep up with their fast-moving pictures. They say that a picture paints a thousand words, and processing visually is much faster than discussing everything with yourself, or checking information out slowly and methodically through your body.

Recognising kinaesthetic mode

People who are processing through their bodies are at the other end of up/down scale. Ask them a question and they will look down, generally towards the hand that they write with, to check out the answer with their feelings. Ask someone a question that involves feelings, and watch as they look for the answer, for example:

- What does a lump of ice feel like?
- What does stroking a cat feel like?
- What does a cold shower feel like?

You may find that some people need to find a picture first (by looking up) before they look down to check their feelings. If they do look up first, ask them if they needed to find a picture before they could access the feelings, and they will be most impressed by your ability to read their minds.

People in kinaesthetic mode will have a much more relaxed, rounded physiology they will talk in a slow, measured way, in a reasonably slow, deep voice; their breathing will be quite slow and it will come from the stomach; while their gestures will be around the chest and stomach area. People who are walking with their feet well turned out will be in kinaesthetic mode - really in touch with the ground and, when they walk up stairs, they will probably put their whole foot on each step.

Recognising auditory mode

People who are processing in sounds will look, as you might expect, from ear to ear. They will probably keep their remembered sounds in the file below the place where they keep their remembered images (see the grid, below); in other words, most right-handed people will look across towards their left ear in order to remember sounds, and towards their right ear to imagine them. Once again, you can test this out by asking questions involving memory, for example:

- What does a police siren sound like?
- What does a brass band sound like?
- What was the last telephone conversation that you had?

Then you could try asking them to imagine sounds, for example:

- What would a singing ant sound like?
- What would be the first thing Madonna would say, if you met her?
- What would Rachmaninov's music sound like on a honky-tonk piano?

and their eyes will probably move to a file below the place where they keep their constructed images.

People in auditory mode may have their heads cocked to one side; they may turn their heads away from you in order to give you their undivided attention through their best ear - generally the right one; they may lean forward to listen to you, or they may lean back with their arms folded (to listen in a more detached way). Their breathing will be in the middle of the chest, their gestures will be around the ears and mouth, and their voices will be melodic and rhythmic. When they are walking, they may have their feet slightly turned out.

I think of auditory mode as using sounds as the medium, which reminds me that everything about it demonstrates a medium between the visual and kinaesthetic indicators.

There is a third auditory file in which people discuss things deeply with themselves: 'Should I do/believe this or not? Yes I should. No I shouldn't.......' This involves looking down, generally to the left with right-handed people. And people who like to talk 'formal English', carefully convoluted sentences with lots of long words and passive tenses, will probably check out their cleverness by looking down and to the left - like Sir Humphrey Appleby in 'Yes, Prime Minister', with those mind-numbing speeches that sent the wretched Mr Hacker straight into trance: for example: 'It has been drawn to my attention that a serious omission has occurred in this instance' - instead of 'You've left out something important'. My mate Caroline calls this 'grown-up language': she has a friend who speaks such grown-up language that she cannot understand a word.

As you will realise, we shift from mode to mode, according to what suits us at the time; and of course the senses are all interconnected. Most people have a favourite system, or combination of two systems, which they prefer to use. We are all different; and you can allow yourself to be fascinated by whatever you discover from the unique individual you are talking to.

Visual construct		Visual recall
Auditory construct		Auditory recall
Kinaesthetic		Auditory internal discussion
right		**left**

Eye-accessing cues for different representational systems
(for most right-handed people)

Imagine that this grid represents the person you are looking at; in other words, your left will be their right and vice versa.

Watch people being interviewed on television and see where they look to find the answers; watch actors and you will discover that they have taken on their roles lock, stock and barrel, unconsciously incorporating everything about the system they would be using in a real situation, including the eye movements. Watch everyone, and have fun discovering the extraordinary diversity you will find.

From My Point of View ....

We can perceive events from different positions. We can do it from inside ourselves - from our own point of view: what we want for ourselves from a given situation and why we want it; we call this 1st Position.

We can perceive something from the other person's point of view - in their shoes, experiencing what it is like to be them: what do they want? We call this 2nd Position.

Or we can be outside the situation, disinterested, detached from either side, observing what is going on; we call this 3rd Position.

Each position has its advantages and disadvantages and, ideally, we need to be able to move freely between all three, and maintain the balance.

1st Position has the qualities of really being who you are, and acting according to the needs, beliefs and values that go with that sense of identity; it is when our 1st Position gets wobbly that we allow ourselves to be talked into doing things that we do not want to do, either for the sake of peace, or because the other person is banking on the fact that we will not be able to stand the feelings of guilt that they are prepared to create.

2nd Position is graceful and kindly; 2nd Position is aware that the other person has needs, beliefs and values too, and honours them. 2nd Position may also mean that we spend our whole lives acting in the best interests of other people, and never have the chance to become ourselves at all.

3rd Position is the detached evaluator - a position for rational input, which every situation needs. The problem with 3rd Position is that, if we spend too much time in it, we can become too detached and unable to experience the emotional needs of either side. Have you ever tried to explain something in which you are passionately involved to someone who maintained their detachment, and found that their aloof voice, their uninvolved bodies, and so on, made you utterly frustrated?

Some of us are very good at 2nd and 3rd Positions, and hopeless at 1st: we have been conditioned that we do not matter; that other people are much more important; and that every viewpoint except our own is valuable.

Some of us are very good at 1st and 3rd Positions: we have been trained to take a detached view of things and so, when we make a decision, we believe that it must be the right one and remain unaware that the other person's map of the world is just as valid as ours.

Some of us are very good at 1st and 2nd and, because we are unaware that there is such a thing as a detached position, we may get stuck in our own and the other person's emotions.

Terence was doing an NLP Practitioner course; he came from a scientific background and, while he was finding NLP utterly fascinating, he was discovering for himself that some of the beliefs that had maintained him throughout his life were no longer valid; as you might expect, all this was coming as a severe shock to his originally well-ordered system.

The students were doing an exercise when I suddenly felt a powerful shiver going down my spine; I turned round slowly and saw, out of the corner of my eye, that Terence was in the group behind me. All seemed to be well, so I left them to finish the exercise and later, over a cup of tea, I told Terence what I had experienced and asked him what had happened. 'Oh! That!' he said, 'Yes. I found myself in 2nd Position for the first time in my life, and I was absolutely terrified'. When I said how much I admired his courage in allowing his world to be turned upside down like this, he said: 'Oh, no! It was my world that was upside down; this is the one that is the right way up'.

The position we are in, in any given situation, helps to create our perception of that situation. Try an experiment, it is called a Meta Mirror, and was developed by Robert Dilts and the late Todd Epstein of the NLP University in California.

Think about somebody you have problems with; maybe he or she gives you a hard time; maybe you feel that you cannot communicate with each other; maybe you have just had a fearful row (let's call that person 'X'). Then stand, as yourself, in 1st Position and imagine that X is standing in front of you. What are you experiencing in this position? What sort of pictures are you seeing in your mind's eye? What sort of sounds are you hearing in your mind's ear? What sort of feelings are you experiencing, and where are you experiencing them? For example, what has happened to your breathing, your heart rate, the level of saliva in your mouth? What is going on in your stomach?

When you have spent enough time in 1st Position to be aware of what is going on, shake *all* that nastiness off and *leave it there*.

Then you can step into X's shoes, into 2nd Position, and just stand there, being X. What do you experience in that position? What is going on inside X in 2nd Position? Describe what you experience as though you were X, standing in front of you, by saying:

I see............. I hear............. I feel

and describe what you observe, *as* X, about yourself: talk about yourself (that person you are now looking at) by name. When you have discovered what is going on inside X, shake *everything* off, *leave it there* and step out of 2nd position.

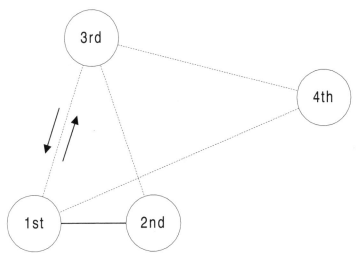

The Meta Mirror

Now step into 3rd Position (see diagram), as far away from 1st and 2nd as you need to be in order to be able to observe what is going on between those two people over there. You are now the detached observer, so fold your arms, and lean back a bit to get yourself into 'detached observer' mode. Describe what is going on between you and X, referring to yourself by name. What is that 'you' doing? What is X doing?

When you have taken in all the information that you need, step out of 3rd Position, and choose a 4th Position, where you can be right outside and observe the relationships between 1st, 2nd and 3rd.

From this position, you can ask yourself what the relationship is between the 'you' in 1st position, and the 'you' in 3rd. For example: are those two 'yous' the same age? Are they the same size? Is one wiser than the other? Is one more vulnerable than the other?

Whatever you discover, you will become aware that the 'you' in 1st Position is probably not the person who is fully able to cope with this situation. And you can ask yourself whether the 'you' in 3rd Position would the right person to deal with X. If the answer is 'yes', collect the 'you' in 3rd Position and take that 'you' back to 1st position, (putting the more vulnerable 'you' in a *very* safe place) and notice how everything has changed.

Then you can leave that 'you' in 1st Position and move into 2nd Position, where you will discover that everything has changed for X, as well. X will discover that this other 'you' cannot be treated is the same way; this other 'you' requires respect.

When you have fully appreciated just how much X has changed as well, shake X off, step back into 1st Position, and enjoy it all over again. (You may find that you would prefer to move, from 4th Position, out into a 5th Position which is even more detached - maybe standing on a chair to give yourself an overview of the situation - and that the 'you' in 4th Position is the person who needs to be in 1st. If so, you can do exactly the same swap with the 'you' in 4th Position.

The Meta Mirror is, for me, one of the most effective ways of sorting out our thinking when we are giving ourselves a hard time. Because we are actually moving from one position to another, it is much easier to separate our thoughts and feelings into their appropriate places, and to discover what belongs where, so that we know what readjustments to make; whereas, if we stay, wrapped in our thoughts, in one position, everything remains in a jumbled, tangled mess and we have no idea where to start.

If I Were in Your Shoes........................

This is about joining someone else in their model of the world; it is very easy if we like the person and really want to understand where they are coming from. If you watch old friends chatting in a café, or a pub or even sitting on a park bench, you will see that their physiologies match each other: they will be sitting in the same way, talking at the same pace and breathing at the same rate. They have created a world of their own.

We can do exactly the same with complete strangers. If you find that you cannot see how they are breathing, all you have to do is to wait until they breathe in deeply, do the same, and then follow their rhythm; interestingly, it is easier to be aware, out of the corner of your eye, of how someone is breathing - rather than by looking straight at them. We can also match or mirror their behaviour, in other words stand, sit or move in the same way as they do and, if they are talking, we can nod slightly every time they accentuate a word. For me, the really magic trick comes from Don Juan, the Yacqui Indian sorcerer, who caught and held the attention of the anthropologist, Carlos Castaneda, so effectively the first time he met him that Castaneda remained with him for five years as an apprentice; Don Juan did this quite simply by looking deep in Castaneda's right eye, and maintaining that contact throughout their discussion. Try it; it works every time, provided that you know that the other person really matters to you.

By listening and watching, we can begin to build up an idea of someone else's internal map of the world. People tell us precisely what is going on inside them, and how they experienced something, by the language that they use. For example, if someone says that everything 'looks black', then blackness is what they are seeing in their mind's eye. If they say that they 'cannot see a way out'; then their internal pictures are not showing them a way out. These expressions are not just catch phrases, people are telling you what is happening - even though they may not be aware of their internal processing at a conscious level.

So there is little point in arguing when someone says that everything '*looks* hopeless'; until they decide to change their internal pictures, everything will continue to look hopeless. It is much more useful to ask 'How do you know that everything looks hopeless?'; in other words, what is that person seeing in his or her mind's eye? You could then ask what they would need to see, to give them hope; and then what would happen if they saw it. If they tell you that everything would be wonderful, and then say that they cannot change their picture, you can point out, gently, that they have just changed it in order to answer your question, and then wonder (out loud) why they went to the trouble of changing it back to the hopeless one again.

*****

As well as telling us what is going on, people will show us *where* it is going on through their gestures. When I was modelling Terence Stamp for *Lazy Learning*, I never had to ask him how he was experiencing anything because he showed me: when he was describing the effect that lists of irregular French verbs had upon him, his hands would come down over his head like a clamp; when he was talking about a particularly important performance he had committed himself to, he described 'this palpable fear', holding a large lump of something solid out in front of him at chest height. As an actor, he is very aware of his internal processing. He was so easy to model, because I could experience everything too, from his words and gestures; some people know, consciously, that something is going on inside them, and some people believe that there is nothing going on in there at all.

A master at joining other people in their models of the world is Robert Dilts who, as a student at the University of California in Santa Cruz, followed Richard and John everywhere and recorded what they said and did in those early days of NLP. I was telling some colleagues about my latest visit to him and Todd Epstein at the NLP University in Santa Cruz: they had done a wonderful piece of work with a woman who was probably less than 5' tall, and what had fascinated me most was that, throughout, Robert had appeared to be about 2" taller than she was. Judith, who is about 5'3", could not understand my fascination: 'Robert's quite small', she said firmly, 'he's only about 2" taller than me'.

He's six foot', I said (I'm 5'8"; with 2" heels, I'm 5'10", and Robert is still 2" taller than me).

'Oh, no!', said the assembled company, dismissively (male and female: average height 5'6"), 'he can't be more than 5'8"'.

And the moral of this story might be: if you want to join someone in their model of the world, in order to lead them to a better place, act as if you are about the same size as they are.

For as long as I have known her, I have admired Caroline's listening skills. In the days when my model of the world was the only right model (and neither Caroline nor I knew anything about NLP), I would hear someone telling her what I considered to be absolute rubbish, and she would sit there, her right elbow on the table, her chin in her hand, gazing deep into their eyes and say: 'How fascinating!' And she was fascinated - she really wanted to know how and why that person had reached that conclusion. Caroline is always surrounded by friends, both male and female, who are longing to talk to her.

The first time I watched Nelda, working with someone else, the only way I could think of describing what I saw was that she was 'locked on'. She is tiny, he was enormous; she was there, just for him, and I felt that neither of them would even notice an earthquake. Both Caroline and Nelda unconsciously use Don Juan's technique of looking deep into the other person's eyes; in listening mode, they do not say much and what they do say comes out slowly, quietly and gently; they match the other person's physiology and then relax their bodies; and so the other person automatically relaxes too, in order to maintain the powerful connection.

Some people might think that gazing into another person's soul could be intrusive; and it is an interesting process to watch. The talker's eyes flash off in search of information from all the different filing systems and, every time they come back from their search, they find that the listener is still there, *looking forward* to hearing what they are going to say. The talker has been so busy searching that he or she has no idea that the listener's eyes have not moved; the talker just knows that someone is there who really wants to listen. They know that because the listener is also modelling their facial expressions, smiling when they smile, frowning when they frown, nodding when they nod and joining into their rhythm.

When I asked Terence Stamp about who he was in relation to other people, he replied: 'Where is the other?' and went on to say that, for there to be another, thought had to be talking, saying: 'she's there, she's different, she's from somewhere else, she's Diana......' and, until that happened, there was no separation. It was a beautiful way of expressing how he joins other people in their model of the world.

Exploring Other People's Realities

Our maps of the world can only be based upon the knowledge that we have available to us; we may have heard a rumour that it is possible to find a pass through this particular mountain range, even though it not marked on the map, and it is up to us to decide how much we are prepared to explore. Another thing about a map is that it is limited, and what will happen if we go off the edge into an area with no guidelines?

Our maps are based on so-called facts, such as: $2 + 2 = 4$; the sun will set in the west tonight and rise in the east tomorrow; if I let this pencil go, it will fall to the ground; they are also based on our beliefs and values: for example, if I do this I will upset X and so, because X matters to me, I will not do it; people like me do not do things like that; this is the 'right' way to do it - I may not like it, but this is what I am supposed to do.

Whatever your map of the world is like, it is your map; you designed it and it has served you well all these years. You know that it has served you well, because you are still here: even if you did get lost occasionally, you found your way back, so you know that your map is reliable. I believe that one of the things that is almost guaranteed to drive us mad is when some know-all comes along and tells us that our map is all wrong, and tries to force the 'right' map upon us, using words like 'should' and 'ought to'.

We may even agree at a conscious level - after all, this person is so much more successful, assertive and self-confident than we are, and he or she was quite right about the fact that we are always late for work/our desk is a mess/ we do not show enough team spirit - whatever. In the meantime, our unconscious mind may be going: 'Hang on! We don't want to be like this person - always so self-satisfied; always pushing other people around; always trying to bend people to their will'. One of my clients went so far as to achieve exam grades just below what was required for a guaranteed place at Cambridge: his headmaster was a Cambridge man and my client considered him to be a pompous, patronising, self-satisfied prig, so there was no way that his unconscious mind was going to allow him to end up like that.

NLP-ers are constantly searching for different maps of the world, to discover how other people have constructed their versions of reality, and how they can borrow useful bits from other people's maps to expand their own.

Let's think about expanding our maps: I have got an underground map of London, because I go everywhere by tube; you have a road map with all the bus routes marked on it; if I want to learn more about London, I can join you, with your map and experience the place in a completely different way, while still able to relate to where I am on my map. You might then like to explore the speed of underground travel during rush hour, as opposed to wasting time sitting helplessly in a traffic jam, or standing for hours in the rain while waiting for an apparently non-existent bus. If we each find that a new map has enriched our lives, we might then go out and invest jointly in an 'A to Z', thus combining three different maps, so that we can really go places together.

Other people's belief systems are fascinating - particularly when they are in complete contrast to our own. For example, if I only have a map of the London Underground, I could be excused for believing that the system was laid out in straight lines (with the exception of the Circle Line, which is not depicted as a circle); or I might believe that all Underground maps were the same, in which case, I would have trouble finding my way around the Paris Metro because, on the Metro, one follows signs to the station at the end of the line, rather than the name of the line itself.

Beliefs have precious little to do with reality: there is the story of the man who demonstrated to his own entire satisfaction that fleas' ears were in their legs. He trained fleas to jump to order; then he pulled their legs off and maintained that, because he had removed their ears, the fleas could now not hear the order and that was why they would not jump. It is how people create their belief systems that is fascinating.

The other person's map of the world is just as valid as yours or mine and, the more different models we experience, the more we enrich our own maps. Should we come across a sign saying: 'Here be dragons', that might make it even more interesting and worth exploring.

Discovering the Structure of Other People's Maps

In order to create a useful change, we need to be able to discover the structure of someone's experience. As we saw earlier, people process information in different ways, and draw their own conclusions from the evidence that they have available. When someone has a problem with, for example, speaking in public, we can ask them one of the most useful NLP questions: 'How do you know you have a problem?'

The information 'I have a problem' has to come from somewhere; it has to come via internal pictures, or sounds, or feelings, or tastes, or smells - or a combination of any or all of them, because there is no other way that we can know anything.

Let's suppose that someone is panicking at the prospect of speaking in public. Maybe he is seeing an ocean of people laughing and pointing at him as though he has got no clothes on; maybe he is hearing assorted voices from his past saying all those things that people say to us as children, to try to stop us from getting too big-headed:

- Who do you think you are?
- What makes you think you are important?
- Who's going to listen to you?
- You're hopeless at this sort of thing

or some embedded commands, like:

- Don't *say anything stupid*
- There's nothing to *be afraid* of
- Don't *worry!*
- Try not to *make the same mistake* as you did last time
- Try to smile, or *they won't like you*
- Try not to *make a fool of yourself*

(These are embedded commands because, if I tell you not to think about apples, you have to think about apples - in order to know what you are not supposed to think about.)

As we discovered earlier, whatever is going on inside us is not reality. If we panic at the thought of public speaking - or anything else - there is something panic-making going on and, whatever it is, it is not reality - it is only our representation of reality: we have created it ourselves. And so we can, of course, create something more useful to replace it: something that will help us to experience what we want to experience at the thought of standing up in public.

With frightening pictures: we can ask ourselves what internal pictures we would like to see instead, and play around with those until we have discovered what would be the best pictures for us to see before and during any presentation we might make. Having decided on the pictures themselves, would we like them large or small, in colour or black and white, moving or still, close to us or far away? And would we like to see ourselves in these pictures, or would we prefer to be part of them; in other words, do we want to watch the movie, or be in the movie? For example, would we like to run a clear, bright, and life-size movie going on in our heads? Would we like to see a guardian angel hovering over us? Would we like to see a sea of smiling, enthusiastic faces with a Tinkerbell flashing about amongst them? We can try out every option we can think of and select the best ones for us.

With internal voices: we can ask ourselves whose voices they are and whether the owners of those voices would really want us to be panicking now, as a result of them - or were they just trying to do their best for us, at the time, according to their limited maps of the world? And this is where we find that they have nothing but our best interests at heart; so now we can ask ourselves what we would like them to say, and how we would like them to say it, in order to support and maintain us throughout the experience. And they will oblige.

For example, you might have a nagging internal voice saying: 'You'll never be able to do this'. So what would happen if you just changed the tone of that voice and turned it into a laughing challenge? Or what would happen if you added the word 'badly', and the voice said: 'You'll never be able to do this badly'? Or if you changed the words to something completely different, like 'You are going to enjoy this, and it's going to be great'?

The feelings' side of panic is fascinating: because we have been encouraged throughout our learning life that logic is all; that we must take a dispassionate view; that emotions are not part of the equation, we have come to believe that this is the only way to think, and thus we repress our feelings. So, when an unusual feeling comes to us, we are rather inclined to shy away from it, without bothering to stop and discover what it is about; and, of course, that feeling is simply a communication so, the more we shy away from it, the stronger it gets and, possibly, the more alarming.

The trick, with a frightening feeling, is to let it out and put it on the wall, or somewhere far enough away from you, to give it enough space to spread itself and play around. Then, when you are comfortable, and it is comfortable, you can ask it what it wants for you; *and it will always be something positive*, so take the time and the space to find out. Maybe it is there to hype you up a bit: to get you on your toes so that you can really get the most from the experience; maybe it is there to remind you that those people out there genuinely want the information you have; maybe it is there just to tell you that it will look after you, whatever happens - who knows? It is your feeling, and you will be able to negotiate with it, so that both of you are comfortable - before you take it back inside you, with the appreciation of what it has been trying to do for you.

And then, just for fun; just to make the experience of public speaking even more rewarding, you can decide which wonderful smell or smells you would like to have in your nostrils - maybe new-mown hay, freshly-baked bread, an early-morning June rose, the earth after a rain storm - whatever favourite smells you have; so that each time you breathe in you will know that this is a place you enjoy being in. And you might also like to allow your mouth to fill with saliva - adding a favourite taste if you feel like it.

Another occasion when the perennial NLP question 'How do you know?' comes in useful is when people have been using the dangerous art of mind-reading: 'You say that your boss despises you; how do you know that?' produces an answer that we can work with - rather than 'I am sure she doesn't', which is just my belief system standing up to yours.

If the answer to 'how do you know?' is because she looks away from you when you talk to her, this may be because she is doing you the courtesy of directing her main learning channel towards you, ie her best ear. Whatever your evidence, if we stop to think about it, we realise that the statement;

does not look at me = despises me

does not equate. What has happened is that, somewhere along the line, that weird connection has been made and is now perceived, unquestioningly, as the truth - whereas, the closest we can get to the truth in this situation is the fact that your boss does not look at you when you are talking to her: this is all that we know, no more, no less. The rest is mind-reading.

If, rather than mind-reading, we keep asking the question 'How do you know?' we will discover endless, helpful information on which to build our knowledge of the situation. How do you know that you do not like so-and-so? How do you know that you hate dealing with your paperwork? How do you know that you are frightened of dogs?

The final answer has to come from inside the person who has made this statement; they may say 'because they bark', so how do they know that they do not like it when they bark? Maybe the sound conjures up a film that they once saw about a rabid dog, just after they had been bitten by a dog, and they are now seeing frightening internal pictures and experiencing feelings of terror. Who knows? We are all different: anything may be happening; and, as we now know, we have created our internal experiences ourselves, and we can change them and create something completely new and more useful.

How Language Can Mess Us About

"But 'glory' doesn't mean 'a nice knockdown argument'," Alice objected.

"When I use a word," Humpty Dumpty said, in rather a scornful tone, *"it means just what I choose it to mean - neither more nor less."*

"The question is," said Alice, *"whether you can make words mean so many different things."*

"The question is," said Humpty Dumpty, *"which is to be master - that's all."*

- Lewis Carroll: *Through the Looking Glass*

Rather like the programs that our brains have created to save us time and effort, the language that we use has become very refined: in order to simplify our thinking, we delete, distort and generalise information; and this very simplification can lead us into quagmires of thought. John Grinder, as a Professor of Linguistics, knew how language worked, and he and Richard Bandler developed *The Meta Model* for discovering precisely what people mean by what they say.

Deletion

We delete information which may be very important, for example: *it would be better not to complain* (this is a particularly British deletion). The soup was cold, the main course was inedible, the wine was corked, the staff were rude and the bill is outrageous. We will probably be brooding about this meal for days, which won't do our health and temper any good, and yet the perennial internal voice tells us that it would be better not to complain.

Better than what, for goodness sake? If we stop and ask ourselves this question, we might come up with an answer that will help us to stand up for our rights. Some more examples of leaving out important information:

I shouldn't get so upset about it. Who says that you shouldn't get so upset? You have every right to be as upset as you like, before you let it all go.

I can't tell him to get lost. What stops you from telling him to get lost? What would happen if you did?

These are all useful questions to ask ourselves, when we find ourselves stuck in a situation that is not doing us any good. Try asking other people the same questions: you will be surprised by how much it will help them to clarify their thoughts. I asked a client who had worked herself into a frenzy at the possibility of failing her exams: 'What would happen if you did?' There was a long pause, while she digested this question; then she took a deep breath, grinned at me and said: 'Absolutely nothing! It's amazing - I've never thought about it. Now I can relax!' She went on to get 'A' grades.

Distortion

Distortion happens when we turn a verb into a noun: an action into a thing. Chaucer and Shakespeare maintain that 'love is blind', and the question is, what do they actually mean by 'love'? Do they mean that, when we are in love, or when we love someone, we do not notice the loved one's faults; do they mean that we do not make judgements about our beloved; do they mean that we see the whole world through rose-coloured glasses, when we are in love; or do they mean something completely different? One thing is for sure: we are not meant to take the statement at face value.

Nominalisations can mean all things to all men. We can interpret what is said in our own way and react to it in whatever way we choose, according to our map of the world - and our maps may be wildly different and lead to surprises for example: when I was about 20, I told a boyfriend that a cynic was someone who knew the price of everything and the value of nothing; and then, because I am not into plagiarism, I admitted that I had stolen it from Oscar Wilde. He went berserk: how could I read Wilde? Wilde was depraved and disgusting, and I must be depraved and disgusting to read him. On and on he raved, unable to hear me saying that I enjoyed Wilde because he was so funny. I discovered subsequently (after we had parted) that he had never read Wilde in his life; his map of the world simply contained all the prejudices of his parents' generation surrounding the Wilde scandal.

More recently, I was working with a GP who listed graphology among 'the works of the devil'. Surprised, I said that all I knew about graphology was that it was the unconscious mind expressing itself through the end of a pen. 'Oh!', he said, 'is that what it is? I'll cross it off my list in that case'.

Nominalisations are slippery because your definition of a particular word may well not be the same as mine; so you and I can chatter away, believing that we have understood one another, and subsequently discover to our cost that we are poles apart when we come to the final analysis. What do you mean by love? Do you mean slavish devotion/complete honesty/knowing what your loved one wants before they tell you? And, come to that, what do you mean by complete honesty? Do you mean telling people that they are idiots, if that is how they appear; or that you don't like their clothes/children/house?

Because we are all different, we all have different representations of these concepts. I was working with a couple who both wanted 'a happy married life'; when I asked each of them what they meant by 'a happy married life', I discovered that it was just a concept, and neither of them knew what they meant. When I asked each of them to think a bit more about it, they found it hard to do so: eventually, one came up with 'doing family things together', while the other meant 'having the liberty to do my own thing within the framework of marriage'.

The trick for identifying nominalisations is to ask ourselves 'can I put this into a wheelbarrow?' Can you put *anger, frustration, love, marriage, creativity, enthusiasm, disruption* into a wheelbarrow? If we cannot put whatever it is into a wheelbarrow, we need some more information. Try an experiment:

> Spot the nominalisations in each of the following phrases, and then think of as many interpretations for each as you can. For example, how many ways could you define 'art', and how many ways could you define 'jealous mistress'? Then think of the number of different meanings for each sentence that you could get from every combination.

> *Art is a jealous mistress* - Ralph Waldo Emerson

> *History is more or less bunk* - Henry Ford

> *Conscience does make cowards of us all* - Shakespeare

> *Experience is the name everyone gives to their mistakes* - Oscar Wilde

> *The law is the true embodiment of everything that's excellent* - W S Gilbert

> *Life is a jest* - John Gay

> *What the imagination seizes as beauty must be truth* - John Keats

Generalisation

Instead of saying: 'those things with four legs, two arms and a back which people sit in', we simplify matters by saying 'armchairs'; instead of saying 'grown-up persons of the female sex', we say 'women'. The generalisation game, when extended, can invade our entire conversation and our thinking: '*women are bad drivers*'; '*nobody listens to me*'; '*the French refuse to speak English*'; '*you can't trust anyone these days*', and so on.

Whereas, with a little judicious questioning, for example, of the statement about the French, we discover that, while far more of the French have taken the trouble to learn English than the English have to learn French, the French are even more embarrassed at the possibility of making fools of themselves than the English are, so they find it easier to let the English struggle with French.

The way to deal with generalisation is to ask the perpetrator whether, for example, he has *never* seen a woman driving well for a single moment; whether *every single woman in the world is a bad driver*; whether she has *never, ever,* met anybody that she could trust; whether *nobody in his whole life* has ever listened to a word he said; whether there is no one *in the whole, wide world* who can be trusted. Then the speaker starts to become aware that there are exceptions to this apparently hard and fast rule: we can even suggest spending a day observing women drivers and seeing what conclusion the owner of this generalisation comes to.

Deletion, distortion and generalisation can often create an image of a malign power that has taken control out of our hands, leaving us helpless. *Anger is bad*; *standing up for yourself is wrong*; *voicing your opinion is dangerous*; *questioning another person's authority is not done*, and so on. We get these phrases so embedded in our minds that we come to believe that they are the truth, instead of stopping to think usefully about them, and to draw our own conclusions from the particular case in point.

Here are some useful questions you can to ask in reply to sweeping statements, and curiously formed connections, which will help you to discover the structure of a problem, and help the other person to clarify their thoughts.

'I am depressed' - *how do you know that you are depressed?* (This is a what do you see/hear/feel/taste smell question - not a request for a catalogue of woes.)

- what are you depressed about?

'It is better not to argue'   *- better than what?*
                                 - argue with whom?
                                 - argue about what?

'I shouldn't be thinking about myself'*- who says?*
                                 - what would happen if you did?

'I can't say "No" to her'   *- what stops you?*
                                 - what would happen if you did?

'She is always criticising me' - *always? So every single statement she
                                 has ever has been a criticism of you?*

'He turned away and I was rejected'   *- how did his turning away
                                       reject you?*

We can become very muddled in our thought processes, particularly if the problem is something that we do not bother to think about sensibly: if we have just shoved our thoughts in any old where, without filing them properly, we have no cross-reference system for checking things out and finding the relevant useful information. Because of this internal muddle, Richard and John created the Meta Model as a way of getting people to find their missing information, by asking the sort of questions we have just been thinking about. (You will find more about the Meta Model in 'People at Work' on page 130 - plus a cautionary tale about over-enthusiastic use of it.)

*****

The differences between 'success' and 'failure' in different people are more likely to be found in their individual maps of the world than in any basic abilities: for example, great communicators have a belief installed in their maps that people are endlessly fascinating and delightful; whereas those who believe that the majority of other people are boring and shallow are not likely to win prizes in the communication stakes. People who excel in sport do so because they want to, and because they believe that they can: that there exists the possibility that they can get better and better; that they can achieve what they want to achieve.

Horsemen will tell you that, in order to ride well, you need to start young. And then along came a woman who had only started to ride in her early thirties. She became fascinated by dressage and bought a very high-class dressage horse from a well-known Dutch dealer, whom she asked how long it would take her to get into her national Dressage team. 'Six years', he pronounced, sagaciously. She, unaware that he was joking, believed him implicitly: he was, after all, one of the best-known dealers in dressage horses in the world. And so, within six years, because she believed that this is what would happen, she had her place in the Dressage team.

*****

Because neither your map nor my map is anything more than just a map of reality, we can give ourselves the freedom to explore each other's, and learn different ways of processing information - of making things simpler and much more fun, and anything else that interests us. The more we explore other people's maps, the more varied and interesting our own maps become: ideas and possibilities open up that may never have occurred to us before, and life, the universe and everything become more and more fascinating day by day.

Going off the Edge of the Map

Some people exist safely and happily in the centre of their maps, and do not wish to explore any further: they have all that they need where they are; while some of us are more adventurous, with an irresistible urge for discovery - an insatiable curiosity to know what is out there, to find out what extra delights and knowledge the universe has laid on for our benefit.

As we explore our maps of the world, we may find ourselves getting closer and closer to the edge of what we know. We may even decide to strike out into territory that is not on our map at all, and to move into a world that is completely unknown. The trick here is to orientate ourselves before we start, so that we know how to find our way back. There are various ways of doing this: John Grinder describes how, when he was modelling the Canadian actress, Violette Légère, she said that she was not prepared to switch in and out of different parts away from the theatre, because she used the final curtain as a signal to herself: 'this play is over; you are no longer playing a part; you will now be yourself again.' She had created this piece of symbolism for herself and, without it, she was afraid that she would not be able to come back to 'reality'.

Driving up through the mountains in California one day, when I was in the mood for playing around at the edge, I was listening to Domingo on the radio and I got so carried away that I did not notice the interference caused by the mountains; my companion switched programmes, without any warning, leaving me feeling as though I was half out of my body (I had been following Domingo up to Top C and the radio was retuned just before he hit it; so suddenly there was nothing and nowhere to go). It was not a pleasant experience but the universe, as always, looked after me: when we got back to Santa Cruz, I went for a walk in an effort to bring myself back into my body again and, out in a back street, I suddenly heard the sound of Domingo's voice. I went and stood outside the house where the record was playing, waited until he reached Top C and then settled comfortably back into my body again.

John insists that we all create lifelines for ourselves so that, whenever we decide to explore, we know that we will be safe: the idea of a lifeline conjures up a picture for me of someone exploring in space while attached to the space craft. Because I imagine that this lifeline is attached to the back of my belt, I need something out in front of me to remind me that it is there when I get into trouble, so I have installed John: in my imagination, he pops up to remind me that I can always find my way back when I want to; and sometimes he gives a timely warning that I've gone far enough, and it's time to go back, now.

We learn by exploration, and any explorer will tell you that the trick is to look after your self: to make your own arrangements for your safety before stepping courageously out of your comfort zone.

Life and Mind are Systemic Processes

The main difference between a machine and an organism is that an organism grows, whereas a machine has been constructed; and so, if we are thinking in terms of life and mind, we also need to think in terms of process.

As we saw earlier, the brain affects the body and the body affects the brain, because they are part of the same system; and, if we start looking for systems within the body, we will realise that there are systems within systems, within systems, right down to individual cells; for example, a cell may form part of a muscle, which is a system within a pair of muscles; this pair of muscles is a system within a limb, and the limb is a system within the body.

A system is, by its very nature, self-organising and will always try to maintain its own stability. If we think about someone who has hurt their foot or their leg and is walking with a limp, the rest of the body will try to rebalance itself; and this may well cause discomfort somewhere else, like backache.

If we think about a system outside the self, someone may come home from work in a foul temper, after an awful day, and start shouting; the person who is on the receiving end may shout back, to maintain a balance in the shouting, or curl up into their shell in an attempt to lower their side of the emotion. Whatever happens, one part of the system will react in some way to the other.

I'm a System - You're a System

'So it *is* all in the mind!' said the No 2 of the triumphant polo team as they rode off the ground - grinning from ear to ear - having scored in the first thirty seconds and won their match 4 - 0. I had been called in because they had not won a match all season and were thoroughly depressed. Having won this match, they were deeply aware, at an unconscious level, of how they had done it, but they could not explain it consciously; so, using their own phrase, I devised a metaphor that they could see, hear and play with.

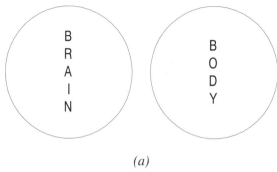

(a)

We have a brain, and we have a body, and sometimes they get separated as in (a), when each wants to do its own thing. When this happens, we demonstrate that we are aware of what is going on at a subconscious level by saying things like: 'I was beside myself'; 'I'm in two minds about this'; 'on the one hand/on the other hand'; 'part of me says....'; 'I must pull myself together', and so on. How often have you reacted to a situation in a totally unsuitable way, and then spent days wondering why on earth you behaved like that?

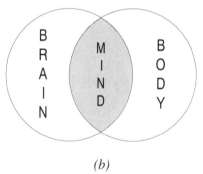

(b)

What I call the mind is when brain and body come together as one system - as in (b), in the space where the two circles overlap. And the question is, how can we bring the two circles so close together that they become one circle?

If we insist, as some people do, upon separating brain and body at an intellectual level, and considering them as two different entities, life gets seriously complicated; and, when we are riding, we have another entity to consider: the horse or pony. So, in a polo team which consists of four players, we find that we have twelve entities to consider, and they may each be doing their own thing, and could be anywhere in the system: see (c).

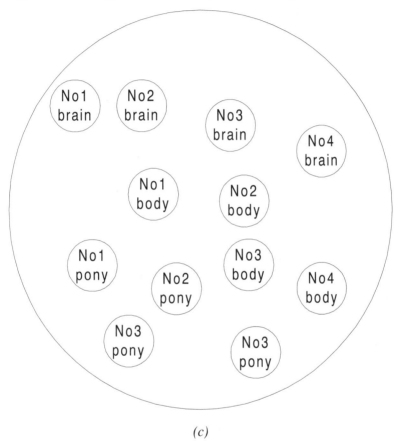

(c)

A team is a system in which each entity plays its own part for the greater system. If we look at the horse/rider system, in the same proportions as the brain/body system, we see that the area of 'mind' becomes even greater; and, the closer we bring the circles, the greater the area of 'mind'. And, if we bring all the circles together, not only do we have maximum mind, but also, we have reduced the number of independent systems from twelve to four: see (d).

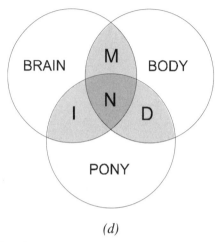

(d)

To create a metaphor for one system, that is to say the team mind, I invested in a paper 'happy birthday' party plate, which I cut into concentric circles:

(e)

(As you will see, the paper plate was rather battered by the time this photograph was taken.)

I then reassembled the plate and turned the concentric circles inside each other, to produced a three-dimensional, independent, gyroscope effect which could move and spin on its own: see (e).

A prerequisite for all this is, of course, our relationship with ourselves, and you will discover more about that in the section on positive intentions.

Understanding What We Notice

There is an enormous amount of information to be gained from noticing the physical changes that take place as a result of internal changes; in other words, noticing how thoughts affects the body.

I love watching Wimbledon on television, and predicting whether a service is going to go in or out. There is generally a close-up of the servers just before they serve and, if you watch for a bit, without looking for anything in particular, you will begin to notice changes: it may be skin colour, it may be shadows around their eyes or below their cheekbones, it may be contours, it may be physiology (the way they hold themselves), it may be anything, because we are all different. What you will discover is recognisable patterns: when you see pattern 'x', the ball will generally go in and, when you see pattern 'y' it will generally go out.

Try an experiment:

> Ask a friend to give you a list of, say, ten people some of whom they like, and some of whom they dislike - make sure that all the people on the list are at one extreme or the other - no half measures. You are going to guess which person falls into which category.

> Ask them to spend a few moments thinking of someone they like and then ask them to do the same with someone they dislike, while you watch what changes take place: not only in the face but also in the body, according to the different emotions they experienced when thinking of each person.

> Then get them to switch their thoughts from one to the other, telling you which one they are thinking of - just saying: 'like' or 'dislike'. Watch them, as they do this, until you can tell the differences: until you have the pattern of the outward expression of their internal experiences.

When you have calibrated which outward signs demonstrate which internal states, go through their list one by one: ask them to think about each person, and then tell them whether they like them or not.

If you want to, you can also ask them afterwards what internal differences they experienced, as they thought about each category. What did they see in their mind's eye? What did they hear in their mind's ear? What did they feel? What did they taste? And what did they smell?

One of the useful results of this experiment is that people become aware of the signals they give off at an unconscious level, which other people will also pick up, at an unconscious level; in other words: if you are doing your best to be polite to Joe Soap, even though you cannot stand him, he will pick up your unconscious signals. And the trick here, if you need to get on with Joe Soap, is to *pretend that you do like him*: try it, and see what happens.

Any and All Communication Forms a System

If you and I are talking, my behaviour is going to affect you, and yours is going to affect me. Let's eliminate visual and kinaesthetic input for a moment and imagine that you are telephoning me to complain about something. If I answer the telephone by shouting: "YES!", in the tone of voice that leads you to believe that I am furious at the disturbance, you will react to what you hear and, as a result, we may be at daggers drawn almost instantly - simply because of the word/words that I chose, and the tone of my voice.

A person cannot not respond to a communication: if X stares at you, stoney-faced, or walks away as though he has not heard you, then that is X's response to the situation.

We talk about having difficulty in 'getting through' to people as though there were some invisible barrier between us; and we say this, because this is what we are experiencing. Maybe the other person imagines themselves imprisoned in their world; maybe they have created a barrier for their protection or maybe we have created our own barrier for our protection. We say 'it's like talking to a brick wall'; 'I couldn't get the message across'; 'she didn't take it in', which are precise descriptions of what we experience - if we stop to think about it.

At the other end of the scale, we talk about being 'close' to someone; we say 'he is very open'; 'she is on my side'; that 'there is something between them'; that we feel 'connected' to 'in with', 'hand in glove with' or 'at one with' someone. We describe people as being 'warm' or 'cold'; 'soft' or 'hard' hearted; we say that they have 'open' or 'closed' minds. What other descriptions (of people you think you can or cannot talk to) can you think of?

And so, with all this in mind, let's think about some other people we might have difficulty with. For example, is there a certain tone of voice that you react to? In my family, we spoke reasonably quietly unless we were angry and so, if someone raises their voice to me, it takes me straight back to angry family scenes and I feel uncomfortable at once. In my husband's family, on the other hand, raised voices were the norm; so, to him, they are much less threatening than they are to me.

There are all sorts of automatic programs that we run in response to the stimuli that we received in our youth. We may see, hear, taste, smell something that reminds us of good times or bad times. Autumn is probably my favourite season and yet, when I smell a certain autumnal smell, I am transported straight back to the hated reincarceration at school after the long summer holidays. Certain words may trigger certain reactions in us: somebody pointing a finger at us may remind us of someone overpowering who frightened us when we were young. I was terrified by a pug when I was very small and, for years, I imagined that pugs were enormous; now that I am 5' 8" it is difficult to imagine how I could have been terrified by something so small. The trick with automatic programs which produce reactions that we could do without is to discover what is triggering off the program.

For example:

> Think about a situation when you reacted in some unexpected way, and wish that you had not; or a situation where you often react in inappropriate ways and wish that you had some choices of behaviour.
>
> Then put the whole scene onto a video cassette in your imagination.
>
> You can now imagine that you are going to watch the video, and it is just a video - something that you can only see and hear.

Then settle back into a comfortable chair in front of your television, to observe, as the film director, how the actors on the screen are going to behave.

Run the scene through on the screen and see the actor who is playing your part, from a distance. Watch how that actor is behaving, and how the other people are behaving; and notice, from this distance how interesting it is to observe the whole thing from the outside.

And, as you listen and watch, you will become aware of what has, until now, triggered the unwanted reaction in that actor on the screen. And you may also become aware how that actor's behaviour is affecting the other person's, and of how the other person's behaviour is affecting the actor who is playing you; and of how each behaviour is probably making the other worse.

Now is the time to take over as director and tell the actor who is playing you on the screen what to think and what to believe, in order to have choices of reactions: how to behave in different ways which would be more appropriate in this situation. Actors are so flexible and creative that, once you put an idea into their heads, they will involve their whole beings in playing with different interpretations, until they find something that works.

Allow the actor to try all sorts of behaviours and watch the reactions of the other people as the different scenes are played through. And then you can choose the scene that produces the precise effect that you would like, leaving the actor free to use any of the other useful ideas, whenever they might come in handy.

And then you might like to step into the scene and play it yourself, and discover how much everything has changed; how easy it has all become and how much simpler life is when you have a series of choices.

Presuppositions and Communication

There are all sorts of things that can affect our communication with other people, and one of the most important is how we feel, according to what we think we know about the other person.

Try this experiment with your family, or with a group - divided into pairs: A's and B's. This exercise is even more interesting if you do it with someone you do not already know.

Part I

Give each group separate instructions, so that no one knows what their partners have been told.

Instructions for both groups:

You arrive at a party which you have been looking forward to for some time, and you discover the other half of your pair, whom you have not seen for years. Talk for ten minutes, and then write down your impressions of the other person - just a brief description: a list of adjectives will do.

Part II

Instructions for A:

You have been asked to a party, which you don't want to go to, but you could not think up a reasonable excuse. You have had a long, tiring day, and all you want to do is to go home and go to bed.

You are introduced to B who, as a much older pupil at your school, made your life a misery. B does not recognise you. Talk for ten minutes (without letting B know that you recognise him or her) and then write down your impressions, as above.

Instructions for B:

You have been asked to a party, which you don't want to go to, but you could not think up a reasonable excuse. You feel out of place and uncomfortable and are planning to leave as soon as you decently can. You are introduced to A, whose name you recognise at once as the person who blocked your application for the job that you really wanted (and which you could have done standing on your head), even though he or she had never met you, and knew nothing of the quality of your work. Talk for ten minutes (about anything other than that job) and then write down your impressions, as above.

Then compare your two impressions, and you will become aware that the differences are purely as a result of the disinformation that people were fed before they started; and you will also realise that the two different impressions that you had were of the same person - the person you did the exercise with.

Try another experiment with a couple of friends, or with a group:

Instructions for A:

You have just started work in a new company, in a very junior position, and you have been invited by your most favourite person in the world to spend a fortnight in your favourite place, or somewhere that you have always wanted to go. You are not entitled to any time off until you have been with the company for another three months, but this is an offer you are not prepared to turn down. Go and see the new Personnel Officer and discuss the question.

The Personnel Officer's secretary, who is a friend of yours, warns you that, however oddly the PO might behave, he or she is really a very sympathetic person who has nothing but your best interests at heart, and that it is company policy to bend over backwards to look after employees' interests.

Instructions for B:

You have just discovered that, since this employee was taken on, the company has heard via the grapevine that he or she has taken several other companies for a ride; so, whatever it is that he or she wants, treat it with extreme suspicion and do not allow yourself to be bamboozled into anything.

What happens? After the experiment is over, ask both A and B what they experienced when talking to each other. How did they feel about the other person; what did they think that the other person felt about them? And anything else they noticed in the course of the conversation. When you have all the information, then you can tell each of them what you told the other about them.

As you will have discovered from both of these exercise, the effectiveness of our communication depends largely upon our internal state: what are we thinking about the other person? What pictures are we seeing in our mind's eye? What sounds are we hearing in our mind's ear? And what is going on inside our bodies: in our stomach, our breathing, heart rate, level of saliva?

The Meaning of the Communication is the Response that You Get

Having experienced all forms of communication as a system, we move on to another NLP presupposition. If I ask you to take a letter to the post for me and you have an immediate humour failure, then my communication has not worked: there was something about the way that I asked you that created the humour failure.

All I meant was: if you happen to be passing a letterbox in the course of your perambulations, it would be a great help if you could take my letter with you, and here you are - giving me a hard time. So, what was it that I said or did that created this reaction in you? Was I standing over you in threatening way? Was I pointing my finger at you? Did I trap you in a corner while making my request? Or was it the tone of my voice? Or the words that I used? Whatever it was, it did not produce the response that I wanted, so there is something I need to learn from the situation.

The easiest way to discover what I need to learn is for me to go out to 3rd Position - like we did in the Meta Mirror - and observe the scene from the outside; then I can see and hear, from a detached position, exactly what went on. I can also play around with different behaviours, as the director of the scene, to discover what would be a more appropriate way to achieve my outcome.

Family Gripes

In sitcoms, family members seem to deal with their gripes about one another in an easy effortless manner - no passionate, personal vindictiveness about squeezing the toothpaste from the middle of the tube for them. Whereas, in real life, things can well be different and painful, as we allow our emotions to get involved, and imagine that a bent tube of toothpaste is a deliberate insult.

A family system for dealing with gripes is very useful; it you have not already got one, call a family conference when everyone is in a good mood and create a system which everybody can enjoy.

My husband has invented an excellent way of carping about things that drive us mad about each other's behaviour, which we now all use; for example:

'I wonder if we could we come to an arrangement whereby the top of the cooker gets cleaned more often.'

'I thought we had come to an arrangement whereby you hosed the mud off the dog, and dried it, before letting it into the house.'

What this system of communication does is to separate the behaviour from the person; in other words, these conversations could have gone: 'You are an absolute slut: this kitchen is a tip! What would anyone think if they walked in here now?' Or 'How many times have I told you not to bring the dog in covered in mud? Look at the mess that I'm going to have to clear up! You just don't care about me at all!'

Here is a very useful diagram, developed by Robert Dilts and the late Todd Epstein, of the NLP University in California, from the work of Gregory Bateson, the English biologist and thinker whose work forms a useful basis for many disciplines - from NLP to cybernetics.

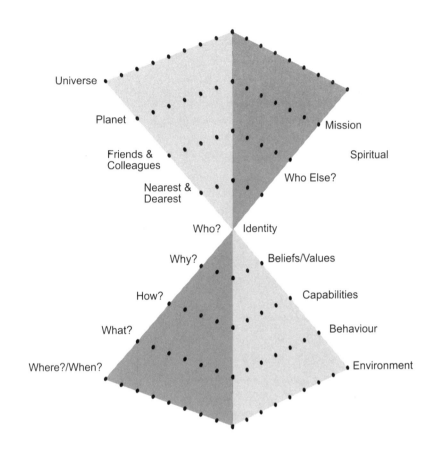

Network of Logical Levels

This diagram helps us to think systemically about what is going on around us; it keeps our thoughts sorted at the different logical levels and stops us from getting into all sorts of muddles about the simplest things. For example, parents often use identity level statements about their children which have nothing to do with their identities at all. They are generally about behaviour, and capability. For example:

You are stupid. This is a statement, using the verb 'to be', followed by an adjective. Grammatically, it is made at identity level.

The trick here is to ask what the statement actually means:
- Did the child let the basin overflow? This was a behaviour.
- Did he spill something? Behaviour.
- Did she fail to answer a question correctly? Capability.
- Does he believe that the earth is flat? Belief.

Whatever answer we get to our question, it has nothing to do with the child's identity. As Noam Chomsky (the American Linguistics Guru) discovered, children know instinctively how grammar works; and, being sensitive creatures, they are apt to take the criticism at its face value, until they learn how to think otherwise.

A useful exercise for making your way around this diagram is to listen to politicians hurling insults at each other, and become aware of how little of what they say has anything to do with logic. As you do this, you will also become aware of how they distract questioners by asking or answering questions at different logical levels. For example:

Q What would your party do to relieve the congestion on the roads?

A As I said in my speech last week, the opposition have been utterly incompetent in their management of the whole transport question: it is high time this country had a change of government, and the efficient road service that the tax-paying motorist deserves.

The politician was asked a simple question at the 'what' level, and has winged off into a 'who' level answer.

If you look at the diagram, you will see that Identity is based on a series of beliefs. For example, someone who classifies themselves as a holistic healer might base this identity on the beliefs that:
- The body is a self-healing device
- That mind and body are a single system
- That the client is an individual, with individual needs

These beliefs will be based on capabilities: things that the person can/has learned to say and do which work, in the healing process, for example:
- Creating a relaxed atmosphere
- Asking the right questions
- Recognising the symptoms

The capabilities are based on behaviours, for example:
- Giving the person their undivided attention

- Giving the person plenty of time
- Listening, without judging

The behaviours will be reinforced by the environment, for example:
- A peaceful consulting room
- A layout where the patient feels comfortable
- Flourishing plants and flowers
- Soothing music

This diagram is particularly useful for checking out what might appear to be criticisms of ourselves: when we realise which logical level they really belong to, we become aware that they are, in fact, just comments on our behaviours, capabilities, and so on, and have nothing to do with who we really are.

Once we have become clear about how our identity is built up, then we can move to the upper part of the diagram, and ask ourselves who we are in relation to our nearest and dearest, then in relation to our wider circle of friends and colleagues, and then what we are doing on this planet and where we fit in to the universe. These are pretty enormous questions but, if we do not know what we want and where we are going, how are we ever going to get there?

*****

The trick with all communication is to establish rapport with the other person, and the simplest way to do this is just to pretend that the other person really matters to you; in other words, you are creating rapport at identity level.

One of my clients did not have any friends at school, so she felt very isolated and, as you might imagine, pretty low in self-esteem. I asked her what would happen if she pretended, just for twenty-four hours, that every person that she came across mattered to her. There was a long silence, and then she said: 'I don't want to do that just for twenty-four hours - I want to do it for a week'. So she did, and everything changed. And, what is more, simply by pretending that all those other people really mattered to her, she discovered that they actually did.

At 'Rapport School' they teach us to match and mirror other people, as we saw earlier. For me, matching and mirroring are just behaviours and, if you do not like, or feel overawed or intimidated by, the other person, then that other person will be aware - consciously or otherwise - that something is missing from your communication, and will react accordingly. If, however, you are in 'you matter to me' mode, then the rapport that you establish will be at identity level. Try it, and see what happens; you might like to use Don Juan's magic and look into their right eye at the same time, as well as matching their breathing.

Because we are all different, we all have different ways of knowing that somebody loves/likes/appreciates/is paying attention to us; and the evidence that we use may have precious little to do with reality. Some people, for example, cannot hold a conversation without eye contact; other people hate eye contact, and consider it an invasion of their privacy. It is worth asking ourselves what our evidence procedure is, and asking other people what theirs is may produce some other interesting ideas.

I once needed help from 'Big Joe', the powerful head of an enormous family of Irish travellers: I had difficulty in tracking him down and I was not at all sure that, even if I did succeed in finding him, I would be granted an audience. When I arrived, I was greeted with politeness, but definite reserve, by his nephew and I got the impression that my story had better be a good one. As I told it, he did not look at me once (and I need eye contact - it is part of my evidence procedure). Once upon a time, I would probably have ground to a floundering halt, but I was aware throughout that what he was, in fact, doing was paying me the courtesy of giving me his undivided attention through his best ear: he listened to the whole thing without interruption, decided my credentials were all right, and then told me that his uncle would be back in ten minutes, if I would like to wait.

Because we are very inclined to do a lot of unhelpful mind-reading when things do not turn out as we expect, NLP-ers are always asking the question: 'how do you know?' We are always searching for evidence. For example, if I had decided that Big Joe's nephew did not like/trust me (which I might well have done once upon a time), the only evidence I would have had would be 'because he did not look at me' - nothing else. And, if we think about it:

does not look at me = does not like/trust me

is another statement which does not equate; so it is always useful to ask our-selves how we know something, and to realise the difference between mind-reading and hard evidence.

Another problem with communication is mixed messages: when a per-son says one thing and feels another; when the words that we hear do not match the speaker's physiology. When this happens, we do not know how to react: we are getting two conflicting messages and we do not know which one to respond to. Imagine, for example, that you were looking forward to a quiet evening at home after a long, exhausting day, and I was trying to drag you out to do something that you hate: if you gave in to me, just to keep the peace, part of you would still be strongly resenting the idea and, if I did not pick up the subconscious signals you were sending, I might live to regret it.

Here is a very useful exercise for not allowing yourself to be bamboozled into things that you do not want to do, or to be talked out of things that you do want to do - just for the sake of peace. You will need someone else to help you.

Stand with your feet parallel and 9" - 12" apart, so that you are com-fortably balanced, with equal weight on each foot and equal weight on the balls and heels of each foot (like the Queen does when she has to be on her feet for hours); take a deep breath, and be aware - from the top of your head, to the tip of your nose, to the tips of your fingers and the tips of your toes - that not only do you not want to do whatever the other person is suggesting, but also you are not going to do it - what-ever happens. As you do this, allow the top of your head to rise upwards, towards the ceiling, and feel the alignment and commitment to yourself all the way down your spine. Maintain this solid, grounded, relaxed and comfortable physiology while your partner says 'yes' (this is all your partner is allowed to say), and you say 'no'.

Your partner is allowed to go to *any lengths* in order to talk you round, provided only the word 'yes' is used - while you maintain your align-ment and commitment, and continue to say 'no'.

When your partner has given up, ask what he or she experienced. The thing about manipulators is that, the moment they notice a chink in the armour (like guilt), they go for it: and, when there are no chinks, they have nowhere to go - so they give up.

Then try the other side: commit yourself to something and say 'yes', while your partner tries to talk you out of it by saying 'no'.

These exercises are about what you owe to yourself; about being committed to who you are, with the beliefs and values that you hold. The technical term is 'congruence': everything about you is matching what you are saying - the message is clearly understood from the outset, at both the conscious and unconscious level.

Everything that We Do Affects the System We Belong to

We cannot isolate ourselves from our system. There are stories about anthropologists who say that they never got involved with the people they were studying, and so their observations were strictly objective. It does not seem to have occurred to them that their very presence anywhere changes things: imagine someone sitting in a corner while you were working, observing your every move and taking copious notes: and ask yourself whether it would make any difference to how you felt and how you behaved.

When we change nature's arrangements, we can expect problems as well as improvements; for example, the little bridge in our village can no longer cope with all the water that the river carries after heavy rain: the land has been so effectively drained that the river now catches all the water that used to lie in the area - with the result that it builds up above the bridge, and our neighbours' cellars flood after heavy rain. Their house was built long before the land was drained, and was not designed to be invaded by water.

On a political level: the Berlin Wall comes down amid great rejoicing. Germany is at last reunited. What could be better? The whole of Europe is affected, one way or another; the cold war is over and the West suddenly has no 'enemy'; the arms business goes to the wall; armies, world-wide, are reduced in size; thousands of people are out of work - these are just some of the less wonderful results of a joyful event.

On a one-to-one level, A bullies B, because he or she finds a chink in B's armour and, the more the knife goes in, the more satisfied A feels. If B decides that there is no longer a chink in the armour, then A has nowhere to go.

Try bullying somebody verbally, *having already asked them to agree happily with everything you say*, and you will discover that you cannot continue to give them a hard time because there is nowhere to go: the hard time you are trying to create is just falling into a vacuum.

If people bully you, this is a valuable experiment because, once you have experienced what it is like to try to be a bully who gets no satisfying reaction, you will know how your bully will never be able to do it to you again. In other words, if there is no satisfying reaction, there is no point in going on. Bullies are just looking for a reaction to make them feel better: *their bullying is about them, not about you.*

I do a lot of work with people who have to appear in Court and who are terrified of being tripped up by opposing lawyers; and my theory is: *if you are telling the truth, as you experienced it, how can anybody possibly trip you up?* The Court system can be alarming; lawyers have cases to win and will try any trick in the book, from imposing their emotions onto you, to persuading you to admit to something that would be true in a different context, and then pouncing triumphantly upon that admission, as if it proved something.

A trick that my clients use, to excellent effect, is the belief that, whatever happens, and however they may behave, the inquisitor has nothing but their best interests at heart; and so, knowing this, my clients can relax, be themselves, and tell their story in their own way. This means that, if they have not understood a question, or cannot think that fast, they can calmly say so, and the lawyers have to begin again. Alternatively, if they do not think that this will work for them, I act as devil's advocate and give them a seriously hard time about their evidence, before the case comes up. This is a lot of fun: because it's just me, they stay relaxed - and one or both of us frequently has to stop, because we are laughing so much; and then, when they find themselves in the witness box, they look at every interrogator and think: oh, it's just Diana, again, - in disguise - playing devil's advocate: I know this game backwards.

These are classic examples of: change yourself - change the system. Play around with them and discover how much simpler life can be.

*****

When we are creating change, even within ourselves, we need to go out into the future and see what effect our change will have upon our system: how will our nearest and dearest cope, if we decide to take charge of our own lives? We need to understand that our change can be unsettling and confusing for them. For example, if you have always been meek and mild, and done everything you were told, how will your nearest and dearest react to your suddenly standing up for your own opinions? If you have always had an answer for everything, how will your colleagues react if you say: 'I don't know' for a change? If you have always been a dependant stay-at-home, how will your family react to your announcement that you want to travel round the world on your own?

Someone produced an interesting theory that, when children are born, they decide what role they are going to play in the family system; and this makes sense when we consider how different children are, in the same family: we can imagine a new arrival saying: 'well that role's gone, I'll play this one: she's the pretty one - I'll be the clever one; or he's the academic, I'll be the sportsman'.

Hinge and Bracket

I had no intention of having two cats. We had left our beloved Isis in Berlin, with friends, because we thought she was too old to go through quarantine, and we missed having a cat about the place; so I went to a rescue centre to get another one and somehow managed to come home with two. Although not related, they had been brought up in the same cage, and were both very good role players. Each was innocent of any crime, and laid the burden directly at the other's door.

Hinge was a sociable, cheetah-type cat, whereas Bracket was the solitary tiger-type; and they disliked each other intensely. Hinge was athletic; Bracket was clumsy. Hinge was neurotic, Bracket was stable. Hinge seized upon the role of 'favourite cat' and, whenever possible, Bracket would move next door, where she could have the role she wanted: 'only cat'. Hinge was anxious to please, whereas Bracket couldn't give a toss for anybody, and would enjoy deliberately setting up arguments and dramas - just for the fun of it.

When Hinge was run over, everyone was shattered - except Bracket, who now has what she always wanted: the role of 'only cat'. Interestingly, she has also taken on the athletic role - taking giant, accurate leaps for catkind - at the age of nine. The crime rate has gone down to about 5%, because there is now nobody else to blame; but Bracket still couldn't give a toss for anybody: as I write this, she is sitting on the arm of my chair, deliberately annoying the dog - which makes typing very difficult, as the dog keeps leaping up onto both of us.

A useful question to ask ourselves is: 'what role have I chosen to play in this system?' Because, as sure as eggs is eggs, if you have chosen a role, then the rest of the system will adapt to that role. In *Games People Play*, the Psychologist, Eric Berne, describes some roles that you will recognise in other people: The Debtor, who says: '*Look at all I've done for you. You owe me!*'; The Victim, who carries a sign saying: '*Don't Kick Me!*', and then wonders why people do; and a host of others like: '*If it weren't for you*'; '*Look what you made me do*'; '*Why don't you...?*' '*Yes, but...*'. '*Games People Play*' is a very funny, deeply serious book, and is well worth reading, if you are interested in systems within relationships.

The Most Flexible Part of any System will Survive the Longest

This is The Law of Requisite Variety from Cybernetics - the Study of control and self-regulation in machines and living organisms.

The solid part of any system will break before the flexible one does: propellers used to have metal sheer pins, which generally broke, when you hit something; they now have flexible rubber couplings; when a hurricane sweeps across the land, it is the solid trees that will fall, whereas the supple ones will bend with the wind, and survive.

The Normans knew about the necessity for flexibility in building: a friend lives in what Oliver Cromwell left of a castle standing upon volcanic rock above a tidal river. She discovered that the tower and the rest of the castle are not quite attached to each other; this allows the building the flexibility it needs to withstand the constant movement of the rocks, created by the inexorable, twice daily, ebb and flow of the tide.

Lara Ewing, who is an NLP Trainer, illustrates this presupposition beautifully, with regard to human behaviour, by describing a two-year-old who has spotted some favourite sweets at the supermarket checkout and makes a bid for them. Mother has no intention of buying sweets, but the child is infinitely flexible and can *go to any lengths* to get them - even to the extent of screaming until it goes blue in the face, if necessary. It knows, as well as you or I do, that - if it makes enough of a scene, or threatens to die in public - its doting mother will probably not be able to withstand the comments/disapproving looks of the gathering crowd.

Another way of phrasing this useful presupposition is: 'if you always do what you've always done, you'll always get what you've always got'; that is to say: 'if what you are doing isn't working, it's time to try something different'.

Supposing that, every time we buy a pair of shoes, we discover - when we come to wear them - that they are too big. It is time to consider whether buying shoes after a long, hot day's walking, when our feet are swollen, is the best way to do things. What would happen if we tried them on earlier in the day, when our feet were their normal size?

If we are always rude to waiters, and we always get bad service, maybe it is time to wonder about changing the way we treat waiters; if our hair goes frizzy in the rain, maybe it is time to wear a hat when it's raining; if I shout at my staff every time they a mistake, and yet the mistakes go on happening, it is time to handle the situation in a different way; if we always panic at the sight of a spider, then our life is going to be restricted in one way or another.

The trick here is to have lots of choices of behaviours: it is perfectly sensible to retreat rapidly if a tarantula is advancing towards you with evil intent; on the other hand it is a shame not to be able to have a bath for days because the bath is already occupied. It is useful to be able to remove a spider from the bath, whereas picking up tarantulas can be dangerous. If, like me, you were brought up on the maxim 'if you wish to live and thrive, let the spider run alive', and because spiders move like lightning when you try to suggest a change of scene for them, it is also useful to be able to put one in a glass and cover the glass with a piece of paper until you can put the occupant outside: this means that you don't have to touch the spider, and it is under control.

There are endless ways of dealing with spiders in the appropriate fashion - I even go as far as apologising to them when I finally have a humour failure about cobwebs. If I want the flies under control, and they want rent-free accommodation, then spiders and I have to live together. It seems a fair exchange, so we're pretty tolerant of one another; and anyway, by the time I have noticed a cobweb, the flies will have noticed it too - so it is time it went.

We can increase our flexibility by using the different perceptual positions we discovered in the Meta Mirror, where we experienced situations from different points of view; for example, if we wanted to continue with our spider analogy, we could move out to 3rd Position and watch ourselves, in black and white, on a screen, in a scene with a spider in it. This is a fascinating thing to do because - from a detached, uninvolved position - we can notice all sorts of things that we were not aware of before, when we were emotionally involved in what was going on.

For example, we might notice that the person who is us has disturbed the spider, and frightened it; and that the spider sets off immediately for its safe place (in the corner/behind the curtain/under the skirting board) which just happens to be behind us. Although we thought, at the time, that it was coming to attack us, we now see that it is simply running for cover - which is a completely natural thing to do; and, whatever we had done, we would still have been perfectly safe.

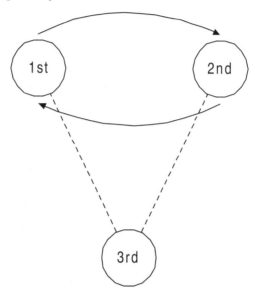

Perceptual Positions

A client was so terrified that birds would get entangled in her hair that she could not bear even to watch them on television. We went back to the first time that she had ever been frightened by a bird: as she had walked into a tiny tool shed, a bird had tried to fly out - each was confused in the confined, dark space and each had probably been just as frightened as the other.

When she moved out to 3rd Position, she was fascinated to observe how carefully the bird had avoided her: even in its panic, it had had the intelligence and the flexibility not to touch her. She replayed the movie again in slow motion, and was full of admiration of the grace and elegance it had managed to maintain while flying in such a difficult situation; she also became deeply aware that, if the bird had touched her at that speed, it would have hurt itself much more than it would have hurt her.

She even chose to go into 2nd Position and become the bird - experiencing its reaction to her sudden arrival; its fear; its need to escape, and its reaction to the lack of available space. And now she derives endless pleasure, just from watching birds, the way that they behave and the way that they react to different situations.

We can use these different perceptual positions anywhere, in any situation that we are puzzled by or having difficulty with. And the trick, with 3rd Position, is to fold our arms and lean back, and become the director of the movie - detached from what is going on, and yet in control of the action.

In this position, we can direct the behaviour of the person in 1st Position and observe how the changes in behaviour affect the situation. We can use our imagination to suggest all sorts of wacky behaviours, to interrupt the pattern that has been created, and in which the actors seem to have got stuck. We can play around endlessly, just to see what results. Imagine what would happen, for example, if the person in 1st Position:

- Resigned
- Told the other person that it was good of them to take such trouble
- Dressed up in a toga
- Addressed the other person through a puppet
- Told the other person to get lost
- Put on a red nose
- Laughed
- Asked for a rise
- Sat on the floor
- Sang a song
- Burst into tears
- Told the truth, as he or she was experiencing it
- Gave the other person a hug

You can be as creative and as silly as you like; you are just experimenting with doing something different - just exploring the endless possibilities to see what changes what. You will be surprised at what you discover; and you will also learn the interesting results of changing your old patterns - and other people's as well.

There is no Failure - only Feedback

It is not because things are difficult that we do not dare; it is because we do not dare that they are difficult. - Seneca (c. 4 BC - AD 65)

Failure

Fear of failure must be one of the greatest brakes on people's hopes and dreams for themselves. Failure could make us objects of ridicule and so it might be simpler to run the program: 'if we do not have a go, we cannot fail and therefore the situation can never arise'.

Because our internal representations of failure may be so unpleasant (perhaps thoughts of failure are accompanied by threatening internal pictures, nagging internal voices and a horrible feeling in the stomach), we may automatically shy away from whatever new idea we may have had, without pausing to wonder what our internal representation is all about. The trick here is to think through the whole concept and, having done that, we can have a greater understanding of what is really stopping us from achieving whatever it is that we want to achieve.

This process follows a series of 'F' words: the first one 'Failure', can conjure up all sorts of nasties inside us, so let us stop for a moment to think what 'failure' actually means - and, as it is another of those nominalisations which we cannot put into a wheelbarrow, it will mean different things to different people. Nominalisations belong in what Gregory Bateson would call 'a sort of conceptual fog', and we need to use our infra-red filters to see what is inside the fog which we have created for ourselves. The question here is, what does 'failure' mean to you? For example: does any of these situations constitute failure in your mind?

- You are learning to ride a bicycle and you fall off
- You did not produce whatever you were supposed to produce on the right day
- You are late for an appointment
- Your relationship is falling apart
- You do not pass your driving test
- You burn the toast

If we think about these situations individually or as a collections of things that did not go according to plan, we will realise that nothing is relevant outside its context. For example, few people would expect us to learn the delicate art of riding a bicycle without making the odd mistake; and it is the mistakes that we make which teach us how not to do things.

If we make a mistake on a bicycle, the body relives the event, feels the movement, feels the balance, or lack of it, and makes its own adjustments for the next time: if we give ourselves a fright, or things do not go according to plan, we learn from what has happened.

If we failed to produce the goods on the right day, we will realise that - somewhere along the line - we miscalculated: maybe we did not realise how long it would take; or the key person in our team was away; or we forgot about the possibility of a rail strike. However we miscalculated, we will know for next time.

If we were late for an appointment - always presupposing that we meant to be there on time - then we were not late on purpose: either we were held up or waylaid by a one-off happening, or we realise that we need to set out earlier next time.

If our relationship is falling apart, whatever we are doing is not working and it's time to try something different; or maybe this relationship has run its course anyway - who knows? Whatever the reason, there is learning in there for us. We shall talk more about relationships later.

If we failed our driving test, maybe our internal state was so awful that we drove like a lunatic or a zombie; maybe we made a mistake; maybe we misappreciated a situation - whatever the reason, there are things to be learned which are going to be useful to us, as drivers, in the future. And, if we burned the toast, we will know how and why we did it, and what we will need to do differently next time.

If we wanted to, we could consider that all these events constituted 'failure' on our part; or we could stand back from them and ask ourselves what we have learned, and also wonder - with interest - how many things in our life we have actually got absolutely right first time.

From the day we are born, we are exploring and experimenting with our environment in order to be able to create some understanding of it in our minds, and to be able to take some control of our lives: when we are learning to feed ourselves, we sometimes miss our mouths; when we are learning to walk, we sometimes fall over; when we are learning how to organise our families into providing what we want, we discover what does and does not work. One thing that we do not do at that age is to create illusions of failure.

It is as we grow older, and are expected to behave in a 'civilised' fashion, that people start to give us a hard time; for example when, out of sheer frustration, we make a scene in the supermarket; we say the wrong thing to Mrs Snoggins; we get a bad school report; we fail our exams; we associate with the 'wrong' people and get into trouble.

All this may reflect badly on our families (in their model of the world); they are embarrassed so they take it out on us. And I believe that it is at this point that we start to get hang-ups about 'failure'.

If we think about it, we realise that it is not the mistake, in itself, that constitutes the concept of failure, but rather the *effect* of the mistake. If, as a learning child, you fall off your bicycle, and no one is watching, it probably couldn't matter less - provided you have not hurt yourself; alternatively, if your proud parents have summoned all the friends and relations in order to demonstrate how brilliantly you ride a bicycle, then your falling off may have a different effect.

The effect of burning the toast also depends upon the context: the kitchen is full of smelly, black smoke and, if you are on your own and not in a rush, you can simply open the window and make some more toast. On the other hand, if the whole family is trying to get off to work or school in a rush, and they are going to be late or go hungry, then they might decide to make a scene about it: you're totally useless - you can't even do a simple thing like making toast properly, and so on - which could result in your feeling a failure.

If your boss expects to lose face as a result of your failing to meet your deadline, then he or she might decide to give you a hard time - which could make you feel like an unreliable worm, if you allowed it to.

If your relationship falls apart, then there is not only your emotional state to cope with, but also what other people (who always seem to think they know better than you do) will say about your failure to make it work.

So I believe that the concept of failure develops as a result of how other people react to any mistake we may make. They are embarrassed or angry and, in order to make themselves feel better they shift the blame onto us: there is nothing really personal about this - they just need to make themselves feel better; there is also the great British penchant for disapproving of success, which creates exultation when people do not achieve what they meant to achieve: like a flock of vultures, there are certain people who wait, with glee, for someone to do something that they can ridicule. Being aware of this, we can let go of all *their* rubbish (which we do not need), then go back to our original mistake, and ask ourselves what feedback we can get from it in order to learn something useful.

Feedback

You burned the toast because, unless the toaster has a fault, it was turned up too high: maybe you, or someone else, turned the knob up by mistake when cleaning it - you will discover whatever it is you need to discover, and learn whatever you need to learn.

If you failed your driving test, you can replay the whole thing in your mind, seeing, hearing, feeling, tasting and smelling what is going on; and you will discover how and why you made the mistake/s that you made, and also what you need to do differently next time.

In order to get a better understanding of that last ghastly row you had with your beloved, you can stand outside it and see what was going on - unemotionally, from a distance; and you will discover not only just how much you were contributing to that row - it takes two to tango - but also what your beloved needs from you. And, once again, you will find out what you need to do differently next time.

Try this trick on an occasion where you once considered that you failed:

Put the incident onto an imaginary video and watch it on your television: you may prefer to have it in black and white - it is your video, you can choose.

From the outside, observe not only that 'you' on the screen, but also the other people, who may be involved or who may be observers.

From the outside, as a disinterested observer, you will discover all sorts of things that you were not aware of at the time. For example, are all those people who you thought had witnessed your humiliation actually paying you any attention at all? Or are they laughing at something completely different?

Whatever you discover, the scene holds all sorts of new information for you.

Fascination

Once we can separate the person from the problem, and the behaviour from the identity (as we did in the Meta Mirror), the feedback turns into fascination.

- Why *did* X behave like that when I said this?
- How did that 'me' over there say it?
- What was that 'me' doing when he or she said it?
- What was going on in X's mind while I was saying it?
- What beliefs must X have in order to react like that?
- Did X take what I said at identity level, when it was meant at behaviour level?
- What do I need to do?

We can ask ourselves all these questions and more, and allow ourselves to become utterly fascinated by the endless variety of human behaviour under different circumstances.

I remember someone being extremely rude to me for no apparent reason. I was shattered, and then, having replayed the scene in my head, I discovered from watching it from the outside - no longer emotionally involved in what was going on - that I had (unintentionally) trapped him in a corner and, because I was taller than him, he was nervous and needed to get out fast. That was a very useful piece of learning, and I have been careful ever since about where I place myself when talking to people.

The fascination continues as we ask ourselves what it is that we want, or wanted to achieve - in other words, why were we doing what we were doing in the first place. Let's go back to the scene in the supermarket when we were young: maybe we saw something interesting on a shelf that we wanted a closer look at - for some reason it was of the utmost importance. However, the grown-ups were in a hurry and had no intention of buying whatever it was anyway; we could not express ourselves sufficiently well to explain that we only wanted to look at it; we could not get our vitally important message across; we tried everything we could think of, but nothing worked, and so we were swept away from what we considered to be the chance of a life-time - screaming with frustration. On top of this, our screaming turned into a failure to behave properly in public as far as our family was concerned; and, what started as an innocent quest, somehow turned into an enormous drama, which the whole family will remember for months/years.

Fun

Once we have got this far, and realised that there is so much to be learned from so-called failure, life turns into a game and, once we know the rules of this game, we can bend or break them to our heart's content. However difficult we may find a situation, we can simply think of it as a game to test our flexibility. For example, if there is someone who has decided that they know how to do your job better than you do, and you know that they haven't got a clue - what they have got is clout - then you have an interesting game to play: you can dance about in all the different positions you played with when you were doing the Meta Mirror; you can dance up and down the different logical levels, and remember always that, if what you are doing is not working, then it is time to try something different.

On the subject of games: NLP-ers only play Win/Win games. We negotiate for the best for everybody. John Grinder tells a story about two old sisters who lived together and detested each other heartily. One day, they were down to their last orange and argued lengthily and bitterly about who should have it until eventually, and with extremely bad grace on both sides, they cut the orange in half. One sister squeezed the juice out of her half and threw away the peel; the other sister grated the peel from her half and threw away the flesh.

And the moral of this story is: if they had discussed what they both wanted from the orange, they could each have had twice as much as they finally got.

We need to be clear about what we want before we start to negotiate; and not only about what we want, but about why we want it. The old sisters only knew that the other wanted the orange; if they had bothered to ask the questions, they would have discovered that one of them wanted a drink of orange juice and the other wanted to make a cake. People want different things for different reasons: one person might want a specific job for the prestige the title brings; another might want it for the salary; another might want it in order to be in a position to create the changes he or she dreams about for the company. All three could have what they want without 'failing' to get the one job.

Another question we need to ask ourselves is: how will we know when we've got it? What is our evidence for success because, if we have no evidence procedure for success, how will we know that we have not failed? Some people have created filters in their perceptions of life whereby they only notice their failures, and are consequently unaware of their successes. You tell them they did something well and they say: 'Yes, but...' We can compare the filters that we create to templates: if I look round my desk through a rectangular template, I will only see the rectangular things on it; I will not see the lamp or the pen pot because they are not rectangular and so, as far as I am concerned, they will not exist.

Bateson maintains that no data are truly 'raw' and that they have all been edited in some way by man - because we cannot get the whole world inside our heads, and thus we have to code information according to our model of that world. For example, if I firmly believe that the English climate is the best in the world, I will welcome the rain as a benefit for my garden, the crops, my skin, the ducks, the water table, and so on; in other words, I will find proof to substantiate my beliefs everywhere I look. If, on the other hand, I am longing for the Californian sunshine, then every drop of English rain could be interpreted as a personal insult.

Planning for Success

So, let us think about what we want, and what that will give us; in other words, let's make sure - before we start - that we really want what we think we want; because, if we know precisely why we want what we want, then we can remain completely committed to pursuing it, if the going gets rough. If you had asked me these questions before my first book, 'Lazy Learning', was published, the answers would have been along these lines:

Start at the bottom of the diagram, and work up.

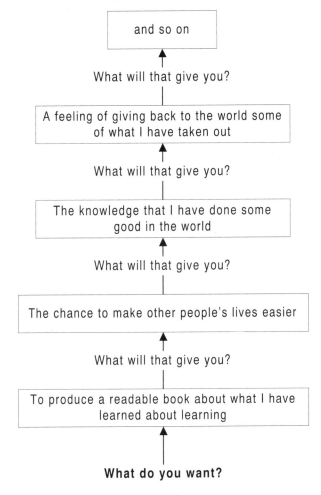

(One of my students - rather irreverently - christened this technique 'The Christmas Tree', and it has been called that ever since.)

And the next question is how will you know when you have got it? In my case, the answer was: 'when I am holding the first copy of the book in my hand' - I phrased it this way because I did not know what the cover would look like.

There will, of course, be various steps along the way, and we need evidence that we have achieved each of these steps, for example:

Steps	Evidence
I have a publisher	I have a letter accepting the book
The contract is signed	I have my copy signed by both parties
The book is finished	I have sent the final manuscript off

and so on

The final question is: 'what is stopping you?' or 'what will you lose if you get it?' In my case, I would lose (along the way) a lot of time with other people, spending it instead in building up my relationship with my computer - which is not the same thing at all, as far as I am concerned. On publication, I might also lose a lot of privacy; but, of course, on the whole, other people are just as respectful of my privacy as I am of theirs. I might also lose some of my friends if they thought my theories were rubbish, as well as credibility within the teaching profession; however, there was a lot I could do to pre-empt this by using appropriate language patterns throughout the book, so that people would not feel challenged or offended.

So, all in all, I was so committed to my mission that I was prepared to put up with the loss of the time which I could be spending with other people. And, as a result of having asked myself all these questions, I could react appropriately in pursuit of my dream, when problems arose. Also, when life was looking difficult, I could check up on my evidence procedures for having achieved the steps along the way, and see how far I had already got: and this would encourage me to continue, because I would know how much closer I was getting to my goal.

What will happen if I fail? This is another useful question and, if we apply it to the Christmas Tree above, we will see that producing the book was only part of a process; and so, if I had failed to find a publisher, I could always try some other ways of helping people to confirm that they were natural-born learners, of creating something that would make me feel I had done some good in the world, and of giving back to the world some of what

I had taken out. Success, as somebody said, is having a fixed goal and a flexible means of getting there.

If we are clear about what we want, about what that will give us, and about what we will lose - before we start on any project, then there will be no hidden agenda from any part of us that does not want, for example, to be rich or famous, and which might pop up and sabotage our efforts; we will be aligned, consciously and unconsciously, with our dream - and anything that does not go according to plan along the way is simply something that we need to learn about, in order to achieve what we want to achieve.

If we believe that the universe is looking after us, all along the way, we can wonder and delight at any setbacks - particularly from further down the line when we discover that such-and-such wonderful thing would never have happened, or we would never have met so-and-so, if everything had gone according to plan. The wonder and delight creates a state of heightened awareness of everything new and exciting that chances to come our way.

Every Behaviour, however Bizarre, has a Positive Intention

As you know, I have a theory that most of us feel pretty inadequate quite a lot of the time: in our society, we have - on the whole - been brought up to believe that we are not important, and that our opinions do not matter; and, at school, telling our peers that they are stupid/silly/useless/horrible seems to be a popular sport. Everywhere we turn, there is someone else who seems to be much better at something than we are: A is taller, B is more elegant, C has a better figure, D is more intelligent, E is more amusing, and so on. As a result, we may struggle frantically to try to demonstrate that we are not the pathetic specimens that we might feel ourselves to be at this moment; and this may involve all sorts of behaviour like withdrawing into our shells; demolishing someone's theory; or sticking metaphorical pins into the pompous idiot who seems to be trying to one-up us at every turn. And we may not, for one moment stop to ask ourselves whether that 'pompous idiot' feels just as inadequate as we do, and whether his or her inflated air might not just be a method of self-protection.

I also believe that most of the problems in the world are caused by these feelings of fear or inadequacy. For example, different nations have different languages and different skin colours; different religions have different beliefs; different communities have different customs, and different families do things differently. In our society, we have been brought up not to be different: we are expected to fit into the mould, to be just like everybody else. As a result, we may find difference to be threatening: your skin is different, your hair is different, your language is different, you behave differently, you have different beliefs - none of this fits my model of the world, so I feel under threat.

I think that our comfort with sameness comes from our need to belong. We need to belong in order to have a built-in support system for ourselves, like our family, our school, our local sports club, our amateur dramatics society, our political party, our culture, our country - whatever we consider to be important enough for us to identify ourselves with.

There is the eternal human paradox which dances between needing to belong and needing to be free to do our own thing: free to express ourselves; free to stand up for what we believe in; for example: when a system we belong to takes an action that we are not prepared to tolerate, we would like the freedom to protest, without the fear of being cut off from our support system.

If we stop to think about it, comfort with sameness does not have to equal discomfort with difference. NLP-ers spend their lives exploring difference in order to enrich their own models of the world. Whoever we are and wherever we come from, nobody is the same as anybody else. You have your way of doing things and I have mine; you have your own belief systems and I have mine - and we may be delighted, bored, fascinated or horrified by each other's.

Don, one of my German teachers, tells the tale about his introduction to Germany, when he went there to study the language. He got off the train, found the bus stop and stood in an orderly, British queue of one, to await the arrival of the next bus. While he was waiting, two elderly widows in deepest black joined him; the bus arrived and then departed swiftly, leaving Don in the gutter and the two old women sailing away towards their destination.

Later, as he got to know the people and country better, he realised that the Germans are not into standing snakes (which is how they refer to queuing) and that, as far as they are concerned, it is every man/woman for themselves. Don was pushed into the gutter - there was nothing personal about this: the widows' positive intention was purely to get onto the bus.

However inappropriately people may behave, it is useful to be able to stand back and ask ourselves about their positive intention. The positive intention is not necessarily towards us: a child who has tantrums may be frustrated at being unable to express him or herself; a burglar may have a family to support; an aggressive person may be frantically trying to protect the frightened person inside; the eternal attention seeker may feel unable to function without external acknowledgement of their worth; eternal attention seekers may also think that any attention, including punishment, is better than none, and consequently continually contrive to get themselves into seemingly endless trouble. The ultimate positive intention is to feel good about yourself. Ask people what their positive intentions are - you'll be amazed at what you discover.

In a nightmare programme on the radio, I heard a now-retired policeman talking about his experiences during the miners' strike, when a mob attacked him, and his female sergeant. It is not surprising that he has never got over the complete feeling of betrayal: *these were his own people and they did their best to kill both of them.* He can also never forget that, when running for help to save his sergeant, who was down and being kicked by the mob, he tried to enlist the aid of a passing motorist - *who just drove on, and left him.*

Thinking about our need to belong, we become aware that man is a pack animal: his large brain realised that he was physically too weak to survive alone, and so he decided to join forces and brains to create an environment in which he could thrive in safety. For example, a man on his own would have difficulty in hunting enough large game to feed himself and his family, at the same time keeping his family safe from predators; whereas, a combination of brains, brawn and expertise makes the whole business of survival much simpler and safer.

The pack instinct returns when we are under threat: we go to war in packs; we howl for people's blood in packs - think how the press stirs up public opinion, or about how we destroy people who threaten our belief systems, like Jesus or Joan of Arc; and think about how schoolchildren can be seen turning in a pack on someone they don't like.

The wretched policeman whom we met earlier did not recognise any of his attackers, and I would prefer to hallucinate that they were outsiders, imported for the day, and that they were terrified - more particularly because the police represent the law, and they saw the two of them as a threat to their reason for being there. I would also prefer to think that the motorist had had too much to drink and so the last thing he would do would be to stop for a policeman. We will probably never know what was going on in any of their minds; but I find it difficult believe that they too did not have their nightmares afterwards.

While we cannot condone some behaviours, if we believe in the positive intention before we start, then the problem becomes much easier to work with; because, having acknowledged the value of that positive intention, we can then look for other ways of achieving the intention in the future.

I was working with a young sportsman who sometimes lost his cool so dramatically that not only did his game go completely to pieces, but also his behaviour was so appalling that the rest of the team's game went to pieces too. We explored the positive intention of this feeling: it was obviously overpowering, so I wanted him to distance himself from it as far as possible, otherwise, we would just make matters worse. People repress their feelings for a good reason: they are afraid that they will explode into something uncontrollable.

I asked what would happen if he took the feeling out of his stomach and put it on the roof of the building on the other side of the yard, so that he could look at it from a safe distance, and discover what it wanted for him. 'It would set the roof on fire', he replied without hesitation. So it was hardly surprising that he would react unreasonably to something inside him that was capable of causing a conflagration (it was not even a thatched roof - it was stone-tiled!).

We let the feeling float up safely into the sky - as far away as was comfortable for him, so that he could find out what it wanted for him, and he discovered that the poor thing's positive intention was simply to stop him from being too relaxed - which was completely commendable: a dozy sportsman is unlikely to play at his best.

So we had two positive intentions: one was to distract himself from the terrible feeling, and the terrible feeling was to keep him on the ball. And, once he had arranged for his unconscious mind to change its wake-up message into something that he could cope with, would understand and *would pay attention to* - rather than a communication that terrified him - all was well.

And, not only was all well, he was delighted to discover that his unconscious mind was looking after him every minute of the day.

Some people who lose their tempers frequently get a high from the surge of adrenalin that happens when they engage their entire bodies in creating a controlled explosion. Their positive intention is simply to feel good (and - if they have never discovered 2nd position - it may simply not occur to them that someone might suffer as a result): this may not be of much comfort to you, if you are on the receiving end, but at least you can reassure yourself that it is about them, and not about you: it is just a behaviour, so you can let go of what you have taken on as an attack upon your identity.

If you are talking about something that I don't know about, I may start to feel inadequate: after all, I'm supposed to be an intelligent woman, and how is it that all this stuff is new to me, and yet you (who seem perfectly ordinary) appear to be so clued up about it? I'm feeling threatened and so, in order to make myself feel safer, I'll search for holes in your argument and then pounce on them with glee. You get frustrated because I keep interrupting and you cannot get your point across: I am not remotely interested in your point - all I want to do is to feel better about myself. That is my positive intention. I have interpreted your behaviour, in talking about a subject that is unfamiliar to me, as a demonstration of a flaw in my identity as 'an intelligent woman' - and that is what I am reacting to: I am simply trying to display that I am much more intelligent than you think by finding fault with what you are saying. Again, there is nothing personal in it: this is about me, not about you.

I was working with a client whose asthma was so bad that he could not hold down a job. His wife was in despair and his in-laws were urging her to leave him and bring the children to live with them. He was at his wits' end.

I discovered that his father, whom he adored, had left the family home when he was very young, and often failed to turn up on the appointed day to see his son. One day, in extreme distress when father had not put in an appearance yet again, he had had a serious asthma attack, and found himself in hospital with his father at his bedside.

'This could be a good wheeze', thought his brain, and tested the theory out the next time father did not turn up; and, sure enough, father came rushing to his bedside again. And so the asthma program was unconsciously filed under 'what to do whenever life gets difficult', and kicked in automatically whenever he found himself under stress.

The intention was positive; we acknowledged and approved it, and then we had the fun of choosing another program to maintain the intention in a way that would be more useful and appropriate. My client decided what choices he would like to have in how to react to stress, and he maintains this variable program - to the satisfaction of both conscious and unconscious minds.

The world of positive intentions is endlessly fascinating; and the useful thing about this presupposition is that we can allow ourselves to wonder about the positive intention, rather than taking the behaviour as an insult. When we are helping people to create changes for themselves, working with the positive intention will ensure that the change will keep them safe from whatever it was that created the problem in the first place.

NLP-ers are always talking about their 'parts': the part of them that wants to be successful; the part that wants to have fun; their organising part; their relaxing part; the part that wants to keep them safe; their sociable part; their anti-social part, and so on. And the important thing about all these parts is that they want nothing but the best for you: how could they possibly want anything else? They are all part of you. And the only problem is that some of them seem to be blissfully unaware of the others' existence.

The trick here is to introduce conflicting parts to each other - with your negotiating part, if you think that's necessary - so that they can sort out their differences by doing the Christmas Tree questions that we saw on page 69. When you are looking for each part's positive intention, you can ask 'what will that give you?, and the answers will take you higher and higher up the logical levels until you discover that they both want the same thing for you, for example: to keep you safe, or for you to be happy, and that is the level at which they will find it easy to negotiate.

They may prefer to do this on their own, if you have got the bossy sort of conscious mind that must interfere with everything - like mine. My parts operate strictly on a 'need to know' basis, which suits us all very well: I don't have to bother, they can negotiate in peace - and they only tell me about things that they think I need to know.

As an example of conflicting parts, let us imagine that Part A picks fights with other people, and Part B hates fights and is utterly miserable. As with the Christmas Tree, start at the bottom and work up.

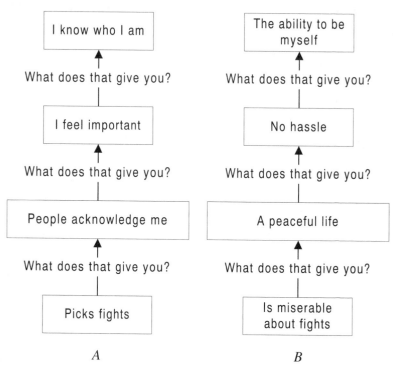

At this level we discover that, like most problems of this nature, this is an identity - rather than a behaviour - question, which needs to be treated with total respect; whereas the person has probably been giving themselves a very hard time about it (and, if he or she hasn't, other people certainly will have done) at the behaviour level - which solves nothing.

We can go on - once again, starting at the bottom:

It is so beautifully simple, when we stop to think about it: at this level, we discover that two apparently totally opposed parts both want exactly the same thing - they are simply striving - in their different ways - to get it.

And this is the level at which we can negotiate; in this instance: how else can you feel good about yourself? What else could you do in order achieve this best of outcomes?

We can use this strategy in any sort of negotiation in order to go for Win/ Win and achieve the best for all concerned; and the question we could ask in this particular instance is: 'what stops you from feeling good about yourself?' - which is also an interesting question linguistically: the use of 'I' and 'myself' presupposes that 'I' and 'myself' are two different creatures. For example: 'I talk to myself': who is 'I'? And who is 'myself'? Could they be your conscious and your unconscious minds?

So, what is stopping us from feeling good about ourselves? Is it the constant battery of other people's opinion? Is it the fact that we do not appear to have many friends? Is it age-old memories of all those things that our elders and betters told us about ourselves when we were young? Is it the memories of the occasional things that we did not achieve in the way we had intended - thereby qualifying us to decide that we were abject failures? There are a million and one things that we could class as reasons - and only the individual will know what the answer is to this particular question.

And more often, when people stop to think properly about what is stopping them from feeling good about themselves, they realise that the answer is: '*Nothing*' - '*absolutely nothing at all*'.

The magic of the positive intentions' presupposition is that nobody can ever be considered to be wrong, bad or flawed - or any of those other high moral tone expressions we hear people flinging about. While we may not approve of or condone the behaviour, we can still acknowledge that each person, and each part of us, is trying to achieve something of the utmost importance.

So, what is your positive intention for giving yourself a hard time?

People Make the Best Choices according to the Information that They have Available to Them at the Time.

Western society appears to thrive on blaming other people for everything that goes wrong: in business, we seem to specialise in finding out whose fault it was, and then sacking them; whereas, in Japan, the ethos is: discover how things went wrong, and make sure this cannot happen again - which seems to be infinitely more sensible: not only because I believe that people do not make mistakes on purpose, but also because everyone can then learn something.

Blaming other people has its advantages: 'it wasn't my fault, it was hers' shifts the burden and the attention (which are the last things I want at the moment) away from me, and onto somebody else. The problem with blame is that it allows us to think that other people are in charge of our brains and thus of our lives; whereas, if we acknowledge to ourselves that we did, or did not, make a mistake, then we can do something about it. For example, we could all choose to blame all our problems upon our parents. Great! Now nothing is our fault, and we can sit back and polish our haloes. However, we now find ourselves stuck in the mould which we believe our parents created and, if they created our reactions, there is nothing that we can do to change them.

Presupposing that people make the best choices available to them at the time creates lots of new options, because it acknowledges the original necessity for whatever behaviour we may want to change. Supposing, for example, your family never stopped asking you questions about what you had been doing, and appeared frequently to disapprove, and to do their best to stop you from doing it again. As a result, you might have decided to answer their questions evasively, to tell lies, or to clam up, in order to keep some private space for yourself. Let's imagine that you chose to answer evasively, and that that behaviour became automatic, and has carried over into your adult life so that, as soon as anyone starts asking you questions, you become evasive, and this is affecting your relationships with other people.

Being evasive when your parents questioned you was the best choice that you had available to you *at that time*. However, times have changed, and you are no longer at their beck and call: you are in charge of your own life, and of doing whatever it is that you want to do. Some of the questions we might ask now are: does *everybody* who asks you questions want to stop you from doing whatever it is you have done or are going to do? Or could they just be interested in you, and want to know more about you? Or do they just need information? Or might they have some useful information for you?

Having realised that there may be a million and one reasons why people ask questions, you can then decide how you would like to react. For example, what would you like to believe about the people who are asking you the questions? What would be the most useful thing you could believe?

And what would happen if you believed that the questioner really liked you, was fascinated by what you'd been doing, and valued your opinion? What changes would happen inside you? And how would these changes affect your responses to their questions?

You can try this trick with any person or situation that you find difficult.

Suppose X always give you a hard time: what would you *really* like to believe about him or her?
- That he desperately wants to get to know you better, but is terrified?
- That you won't pay any attention to him at all unless he is really heavy-handed?
- That all she needs is reassurance from you that she is okay?
- That he would love to behave with kindness and courtesy, he just does not know how to - yet?
- That she believes that you think that you are better than she is?

You know X and I don't - you'll be able to think up all sorts of interesting things to believe about him or her. Try them all on for size, and discover what happens to your internal state; then you can choose the one that you like best, and pretend that that is what you believe, next time you have contact with X. And you will be astonished by what happens - by how everything changes.

Some people will say that they cannot pretend something that is not real - so they could not possibly try on a belief that was not 'true'. This just means that they still believe in 'reality' as something concrete - whereas you and I know that it is an abstract concept, and exists only in our minds; and that our different models of reality may have little in common - although mine is just as real to me as yours is to you. We could, for example, deny the existence of those high-pitched dog whistles - because we cannot hear them; the same goes for an elephant's long distance communications - they are so low-pitched that we cannot hear them. The fact that the sounds are not evident to us does not necessarily mean that they do not exist; an example - for people who do not believe in extra-sensory perception - is the unfortunate man whose dog knows exactly when he leaves his office: so when he gets home from the pub, saying he was delayed at work, neither the dog nor his wife believes him.

It's a shame if we somehow manage to lose the creativity of childhood: that open, aware state when we could believe anything that we wanted to believe to enhance our play: when a cardboard box could become a car, a boat or a treasure chest; when a sheet could become a cloak, a den or a magic carpet. And we all need to remind ourselves, from time to time, that almost everything that we see around us was once a figment of someone's imagination: once upon a time there were no gardens, no computers, no satellites, no 'pedigree' dogs, no Waldorf salads, no chairs, no clocks. All these things were, originally, the figment of someone's imagination: someone 'pretended' that they could exist, and wondered what would happen if they did. They looked forward, into the future, liked what they saw, and set about creating something concrete from their 'pretence'.

If we choose to believe that people are making the best choices available to them, we realise that there is nothing personal about whatever behaviour we do not like: they just need to feel better. In other words: that this behaviour is about them, and not about us.

People Have within Them All the Resources that They Need

We carry with us the wonders we seek without us. There is all Africa and her prodigies in us. - Sir Thomas Browne (1605 - 1682), *Religio Medici.*

In *The Wizard of Oz*, the lion believed that he had no courage, the tin man believed that he had no heart, and the scarecrow believed that he had no brain: it took a visit to the wizard (who believed he was a fraud anyway) for them to discover for themselves that their own beliefs were misplaced.

Supposing that we think that our main problem is that we are not creative: we are surrounded by artists, musicians, poets, designers and think that, if we were like them, all our problems would be solved; but we're not, so that's that.

The trick with resources (because they are nominalisations) is to decide what we actually mean, before we start looking for them. For example, what precisely do you mean by *'courage'*, *'inner strength'*, *'credibility'*, *'self-confidence'* *'creativity'*?

Let's think about creativity for a bit: it comes in many guises. My diction-ary definitions of 'to create' are:

To cause to exist: think of all the things you have caused to exist, for example: meals, which were once just a collection of ingredients which you put together to become something different; friendship, where you did certain things to create something that was not there before; a letter you wrote, which did not exist before you wrote it; your Christmas tree, which was once just a tree and a collection of orna-ments. You will be able to think up dozens more examples for your-self.

To produce: for example, when did you last produce the right word or gesture, at the right moment; a bunch of flowers which you had selected as being appropriate for a particular occasion; something from your garden, or your window box; a compromise between people who are disagreeing; a brilliant idea off the top of your head? - the list could go on for ever.

To originate: you'll be able to find all sorts of things to go in here, like giving a party; creating something new, delicious and unexpected to eat, because you forgot to buy a vital ingredient and had to substitute something else; a new plan for running something; an easy way of doing something; a new way to describe something.

My son Hugo's spelling was described as 'whimsical' at school; and one day, in the car, we were challenged with: 'I spy, with my little eye, something beginning with JKW'. The answer was Dual Carriageway. This delightful piece of creativity went straight into family folklore and now, twenty years on, we still talk about JKWs when giving each other directions.

What sort of things have you originated recently? Stretch your mind and think about it; for example, every sentence that you generate is original to you: you have strung a series of words together to express your own thoughts in your own way; every connection you make with another person is original to you and that person: even picking up the telephone to get a number from Directory Enquiries is something that you originate.

*****

Robert Dilts and the late Todd Epstein, of the NLP University in California, developed the SCORE model, which is an another of their excellent tools for separating our thinking out into the right places.

Symptom

Cause

Outcome

Resources

Effects

There are endless ways of playing with the SCORE, and one of the most important things about it is that we can do each piece of thinking in its own appropriate place, by laying the problem out on the floor:

Cause ------ Symptom [+ Resources] ------ Outcome ------ Effect

the easy way to do this is to write each word on a different piece of paper, and step onto each piece of paper as we go through the different aspects of the problem.

Let's fit a problem into the pattern. Supposing X wants to stop biting his nails: we have the Symptom and the Outcome - which, as you will notice, are the direct opposite of each other:

Symptom: *biting his nails*

Outcome: *not biting his nails*

Once you have got these two, X can stand on the symptom spot, and experience what is going on as he bites his nails: what is he seeing, hearing, feeling, tasting, smelling?

From there, he might like to move back into the Cause space, and discover what is causing him to bite them, or what caused him to develop the habit of biting them, or he might like to step across the Resources space and into the Outcome, to experience what it is like in that space - not biting his nails.

Wherever he chooses to go, we need to be aware that the only person who knows about any aspect of his nailbiting is X - we cannot possibly know what goes on inside him unless he tells us, or shows us; and so imposing our own model of nailbiting will hinder, rather than help, the process.

I like going for the Effect after Outcome and before Cause - where possible, in order to make sure that X really wants this outcome.

X moves into the Effect space, and we ask the question, 'what is the effect, now that you no longer bite your nails? What is happening in this space? What is life like here? What is going on inside you?'

Notice that we are speaking in the present tense, which we will do in every space: in Effect we have moved forward into the future, when the outcome has been achieved; whereas in Cause we move back into the past to relive that moment.

Whichever way round you do Cause and Effect, the important thing to remember is that X needs to be *in* each state, being there, experiencing what is going on. If he starts saying things that do not belong in that state, ask him to step off the line, and observe what is happening to the imaginary X on the line; he can step back into the spot when he is ready to go fully back into the appropriate state again. In other words, keep the different states firmly separated, and make sure that X is talking in the present tense; for example, in

Symptom, X might be saying: 'I am biting my nails; I can feel and hear the click as my teeth go through; I wonder if I can get any more off this one...'

Analysis also belongs outside the line. And so, the moment X starts saying things like: 'People bite their nails because...' or 'you do so and so because so and so' we know that he has moved out of the appropriate state and into analysis, which is not going to solve the problem - if analysis was way to solve this, X would have solved it years ago; so, if this happens, ask him to step off the line again, until he has given full flow to his urge to analyse.

The moment for analysis comes when X has been through and experienced everything from Cause to Effect, through all five senses; then he can stand outside the line and see what resources he needs to get him from Symptom to Outcome.

Let's suppose that self-confidence is the resource that he needs.

This is the fun bit: ask him to go back to a time when he not only felt confident in himself, but also he achieved what he wanted to achieve; ask him to relive that moment and tell you about it, exactly as it is happening: what he is seeing, feeling, hearing, tasting and smelling.

You will notice that, as he relives the moment, his physiology will change; he will stand up straighter and seem to grow; his skin colour will change; the contours round his face will change; his breathing and his voice will change - and you may notice lots of other things as well. If you want to have even more fun, you can ask him to remember other similar occasions, so he has lots of practice at returning to this state.

You then ask him if he would like his own magic button to press, so that he can feel confident whenever he wants to: the magic button could be something like squeezing or rubbing his thumb and forefinger together, or crossing his fingers, or anything he likes (provided it is something that he can do in public, without people sending for the men in white coats).

Then you can ask him to bring back the first moment and - as it comes flooding into his body with all those good feelings - to press his magic button and step into the Resource space, seeing, hearing, feeling, tasting and smelling that moment all over again; then ask him to bring back the second moment, pressing his magic button, then the third, and so on - until the whole of the Resource space seems to be filled with his confidence in himself.

And now comes the best bit:

Ask X to go back into the Cause space, pressing his magic button, so that he is taking this wonderful, confident state back into the past to a time when he really needed it; and he will find that the whole situation in Cause has changed.

When he has truly appreciated the changes, he can move on into the Symptom space, pressing his magic button again, to heighten the confidence; and, once again, he will find that everything has changed.

When he is ready, he can move into the Outcome space - stopping in Resources if he really wants to indulge himself (always, pressing his magic button) - and really know what the outcome is like.

And finally, he can take it all into the Effect space, and just be there, enjoying himself to the full.

Judith DeLozier, to whom this book is dedicated, is a dancer as well as a Co-Developer of NLP, and she had the idea of dancing your way through the SCORE, instead of talking it. Try it; it's wonderful!

*****

Some people may tell you firmly that they have never had a moment's self confidence (or whatever resource it is that they need) in their lives. This requires a more thorough search, which is also a lot of fun. You might have to indulge them by calling self-confidence by another name, like 'feeling okay about yourself', or 'having no worries' or whatever state they decide to choose as being the nearest they think they can get to self-confidence.

This part of the experiment happens along what we call a Timeline; in other words, you ask Y to lay a line out along the ground in her mind's eye, and decide which direction faces the future, where now is, and where the past is.

<pre>
                           N
        Past ───────── N O W ───────── Future
                           W
</pre>

Let's suppose that Y has decided that what she needs is courage in order to stand up for herself, and she thinks that she has never had a moment's courage in her life: ask her to step into the NOW spot, and tell her that she is going to make her way slowly back into the past, and rediscover the moments where she stood up for herself, without even thinking about it - just because it was so much a part of who she was.

You can tell her that she may not even have noticed what she was doing at the time, because it was simply so natural; but that her body will remember every moment.

Then you can ask her to step slowly backwards, into the past, and tell her that her body will know when she has got to a moment where she was quite happy about standing up for something she believed in, and that she will stop in that moment, and relive it.

When she does this, ask her - as you asked X - what she is seeing, hearing, feeling, tasting and smelling, in this moment: as with X, it all needs to be relived in the present tense, and analysis belongs off the line.

Allow Y to move slowly back through time, stopping and savouring what is going on in each moment, and allowing her plenty of time to discover all she needs to discover - until she gets back to her birth.

She may even want to go further back than that. (Should she by chance come to a bit on her timeline that she does not want to go through, she can step over it, walk round it, shine some light on it - whatever she wants to do.)

(When Y gets to a really good moment - when her physiology is now completely different from what it was at the beginning, ask her to come off the line for a bit {when she has really appreciated the moment}, and explain to her about the magic button; then ask her to step back into that moment again and press her button as all that good stuff comes back to her - so that she can reproduce that experience whenever she wants to. Having discovered her magic button, she can now press it as she steps into every good moment.)

When she has got back to the beginning, she can - in her own time - walk forward to the Now spot, stopping once again at all those places she stopped before, and pressing her button to reinforce the state as she relives them again. At this point, it might be interesting to wonder, out loud, how many more of those moments will become apparent to her on the way back, so that she can stop and enjoy them, as well.

When she gets back to NOW, fully aware of just how well she can stand up for what she believes in, she can either take that state into the SCORE model, as X did, or she can walk into the future, into situations where this state may be needed, and see what happens. After she has done this, and appreciated the change, she can then come back to NOW and enjoy her self to the full; and then she can take all these treasures into the SCORE Model, and discover how everything has changed.

As you will have realised, all the resources are there, and just waiting to be rediscovered: some young French clients of mine decided to imagine that all the resources lived on the shelves of our little local shop and so, if they needed anything, they would go to the shop in their imaginations, and just help themselves to whatever they wanted - and to anything else that they fancied, just for good measure.

If you should come across somebody who firmly insists that he has never, ever, in his whole life experienced a particular emotion, there are other ways of approaching it: you can suggest that he just pretend that he has; or, if he is one of those people who cannot pretend, ask him to act 'as if' he has; if he is still determined not to play, you can ask: 'what would happen if you had courage/patience/choices?' The trick with people like this, when they swear blind that such a state has never existed for them, is to ask them why they want it. In other words, how do they know that it will be good for them, if they have never experienced it? How do they know that it will not be even worse than before?

The answer, of course, is that they have already tried the state on for size, and decided that that is what they want. How else could they know? And, as with all our experiments, treat the other person with respect and gentleness - otherwise they might start getting terrified by how brilliantly obliging their brains are.

Part II:
Beyond Presuppositions and into Practicalities

As you discovered earlier, no NLP-er would maintain that any of these presuppositions was true - we just find that having them as the basis for our thinking makes our lives a whole lot simpler, and a whole lot more fun.

Now that you have thought about, and played around with them, the question I would ask is:

What would happen if these presuppositions became yours as well?

What would life be like for you? What changes would they make to the way that you cope with other people and situations? Stop and think about it for a moment: for example, what would you now see, hear, feel, taste and smell when dealing with somebody whom you used to believe was deliberately difficult? Or with someone who seemed to be deliberately messing you around? Or a bully? Or your nearest and dearest? Or a disobedient child? With all this new information, how would you react in situations which you used not to be able to handle particularly well?

NLP, as a unified field theory, can be applied to anything. My main areas of interest are learning, health, relationships, and business, and so I thought it might be useful for you to experiment with some ways of using what you have discovered in these different areas (with the exception of learning, for which you can consult my *Lazy Learning: Making the Most of the Brains You were Born With* - see the Bibliography).

As you will discover, all these fields are interrelated anyway; so the headings in this section are pretty arbitrary. For example, there is a section called 'People at Work (and at Play)': because people are just people, what you use in one situation, you can use in another. For example, as you know, I also do a lot of work with sport and in the Law Courts - neither of which seems, on the surface, to have much to do with my main interests; however - because everything is all about people, and how they function - once you have the presuppositions engrained, all you need to remember is:

1. What is my outcome?
2. What resources do I need?
3. Everyone I come into contact with really matters to me.

For example, one of my clients was appealing against a conviction for a crime he had not committed. Our outcome was clear: that he get off; for external resources we had a Barrister, who did not appear to believe a word of my client's - admittedly unusual - story, and we needed one vital piece of evidence: a photograph, which had mysteriously disappeared from the police station. The internal resources that we needed were commitment to our outcome, and the ability to maintain our internal states, so that we could achieve it in the easiest possible way.

The Barrister was firmly attached to small points of law, and everything - as far as he was concerned - looked bad. (I was aware, here, that he was in visual mode, and he reminded me of a bird, at this stage, pecking punctiliously at little grains of legality.)

And so (gazing deep into his right eye; knowing that this guy really mattered to me; that he had a job to do, and was full of positive intentions; and that he was doing his best according to the information available to him) I joined him in his model of the world (points of law) and asked whether 'innocent until proved guilty' still held good under English Law. It did. I then needed to understand why, in that case, the onus was on us to prove my client's innocence, rather than the other way around, and mentioned that the police had conveniently 'lost' the only evidence that proved him innocent. I was told firmly that, because my client had admitted guilt when in police custody, this was all the proof that was needed - his fear and confusion at the time played no part in the equation.

Fascinated by this curious piece of reasoning, I asked the Barrister whether, if I refused to stop beating him over the head until he promised to marry me, I could then sue him for breach of promise, when he came to his senses. No, I couldn't, he said triumphantly, for breach of promise was no longer an offence under the law.

Then he stopped, for a millisecond, and I knew that my seed had germinated; so I offered to appear in the witness box in my professional capacity (working with victims of serious crime), to discuss the effects of intimidation of witnesses upon their internal states, and their resulting behaviour. This served to unsettle his beliefs about my client's guilt yet further (he had disregarded my presence so completely that, when I was introduced - by name only - he asked my client: 'Would she like to go and find a cup of coffee while we talk?'), because he did not know that I was there in any professional capacity. He must have realised at this point that the very fact that I had been called in demonstrated that my client meant business.

Where possible, I like to work in large chunks; in other words, I like to go way up the levels to an overall view, rather than mess around with small detail - hence my first question: 'innocent until proved guilty?'; the Barrister was a small chunk man, and not comfortable with my large chunk questions. He escaped as soon as he could, and left us to our own devices.

What seemed like hours later, he reappeared, looking quite different. His small chunk brain had been busy and he had made a fascinating discovery. There were three witnesses for the prosecution: a woman who had reported the incident, and two policemen who had arrested my client. On the day my client had been convicted, the woman made a statement describing the man she had seen as well-dressed, in a collar and tie and a tweed jacket, with 'unkept' (sic) greying hair. One policeman described my client (the man he had arrested), accurately, as scruffily dressed in sweatshirt and jeans, with dark hair; the other one described him as smartly dressed in a jacket, collar and tie. With two contradictory stories, it was this second policeman whom the magistrates had chosen to believe. What the Barrister had discovered was that this policeman had lifted his written statement, in its entirety, from the witness's written statement - even to the extent of copying her misspelling of 'unkempt' - would you believe!

Learned Counsel had changed from a bird into a terrier: he had smelled blood, and nothing was going to stop him from following his nose, until he found the source. He had had words with the prosecutor and the judge - both of whom had agreed immediately that this case, as it appeared, would not stand up for a minute. It was adjourned on the understanding that, when the police photograph was found and, if it showed what my client said it showed (ie himself scruffily dressed in jeans and a sweatshirt), the whole thing would be dropped.

And the moral of this story is: we need input from both large and small chunk thinkers; and, if we can have the flexibility to think in both ways ourselves - from the big picture to the fine detail, and back again - then life gets easier still.

In the next section you will be able to experiment with some more of the techniques which have evolved from the presuppositions we have been talking about: you will be able to invent lots more for yourself. It is just a matter of experimenting, and asking ourselves questions based upon our presuppositions, such as:

- What might X's positive intention be?
- If Y got this response to that communication, what could he do differently?
- What can I learn from this mess?
- What would have to be 'true' for Z, if she behaves in this way?
- How is what A is doing affecting the system ABC?
- How can I understand B's model of the world better?
- How is C's belief system affecting his health?
- What resources does D need?
- What does E need to believe in order to succeed?
- How can I increase my choices in this situation?

And, if we want to know what is really going on inside somebody else, rather than mind-reading - which is notoriously inaccurate - the simplest thing to do is to ask.

If We had World Enough and Time................

Time is a man-made device. The universe does its own thing, in its own rhythms, while we rush around frenetically - watching the clocks, which we invented.

How We Organise Time

This section is about how we have organised the concept of time in our brains. Remember, you had no handbook when you were born; you programmed your own brain, all by yourself; and, because they are your programs, you can change and update them in any way that you want.

Where do you keep the past, the present and the future in your mind's eye? How do you know which is which? In other words, how do you know when you have done something, or whether it's still just a plan?

Some people know exactly how they know; others produce answers like: 'I just do'. Some people will *tell* you how they have organised time: they will talk about 'planning ahead' and 'looking forward' to something, and you will know that they see the future somewhere in front of them; or they will say things like: 'I put it behind me', and 'I never look back', which will tell you that they keep the past somewhere behind them.

To find out how someone has organised time, you can ask them these questions.

- What were you doing this time last year?
- What were you doing this time last month?
- What were you doing this time last week?
- What were you doing yesterday?
- What are your plans for tomorrow?
- What are your plans for this time next week?
- What are your plans for this time next month?
- What are your plans for this time next year?

If you visualise all these events in your mind's eye, you will become aware that you have organised them in a particular way. For example, how can you tell which picture represents what you were doing yesterday rather than what you were doing last week, or what you will be doing tomorrow? There must be millions of variations; some examples of general organisation of time: most right-handed people see the past on the left and the future on the right - set out in various different ways, for example:

(a)

Past ————— Present ————— Future

or (b):

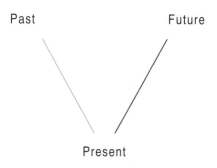

or (c):

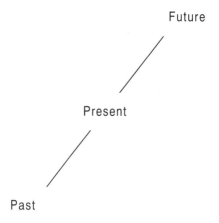

whereas left-handed people might have reversed versions of these patterns. You can also discover whether people are left/righters or right/lefters by asking them the same sort of questions that we asked when we were looking at eye-accessing cues on page 12, for the past, and see which ways their eyes move before they answer. Then you can ask them about their plans for the future, and watch their eyes again.

Some people perceive time on a straight back to front line:

(d)

Future

Present

Past

Some people have it laid out like an annual planner in a diary, and some perceive it as circular or oval, maybe year on year. As with everything else, we are all different, and there is no 'right' or 'wrong' way; the question is: is the way you have organised time useful for you? For example, I decided that one timeline was not enough; I needed two: one for living in, and one for planning. My planning line runs from left to right, in front of me, and has all the learnings I have selected from the past, while all the rubbish from my past - which I no longer need - is behind me.

People whose timelines run from right to left - the opposite of (a) above - may find reading and writing difficult: because we read from left to right, the past (what we have read) is on our left, and the future (what we are about to read) is on our right; and so, if we have got past and future programmed the other way round, reading and writing might well be confusing. If this situation applies to you, and you would rather have your past on your left, you will find that your brain is totally adaptable: just explain what you want, and ask it to switch.

A young client of mine suddenly found that his schoolwork was going downhill: I asked what changes had happened just before this, and discovered that he had started to read the Koran. His brain had made the switch in order to read from right to left, and had not realised that it needed to switch back again for English.

I also know lots of people who have right/left timelines and have never had any problem with reading or writing.

People who keep the past in front of them and the future behind them may find it difficult to make plans, because they literally have nothing to look forward to.

On the subject of looking forward to things: 'disappointment requires adequate planning', is one of Richard Bandler's classic one-liners. Think about it, and about how you can plan for success, instead.

People whose time is all organised in front of them in a very narrow V may

(e)

P   F
a   u
s   t
t   u
       r
       e

Present

find that they keep on making the same mistakes, over and over again - because they find it hard to distinguish between what has happened and what they are planning: Sir Arthur Strebe-Grebeling (alias one of my favourite comedians, the late Peter Cook) put this very well: he learned from his mistakes and could repeat them exactly.

The advice 'put it all behind you' is sound: when someone is plagued by bad memories, they have probably got them in pictures in front of them, as a permanent reminder for them to feel bad. If they don't want to keep the past behind them, they can just make the pictures smaller, fuzzy, black and white - or move them further away - whatever it needs to put those events into proportion with the here and now.

The Deadline is Looming!

Another way we give ourselves a hard time, and pile on the stress is when enormous, threatening pictures come up at us to remind us that we need to have done something SOON! When this happens, it is just your unconscious mind keeping you on the ball: you can thank it for the reminder, and move the picture further away, to somewhere that is comfortable for you but will still keep you on schedule. My father kept his deadlines much closer than I did, and used to drive me mad by asking me why I wasn't ready - when we weren't scheduled to leave for half an hour. He was a bit like Uncle Matthew in Nancy Mitford's *Pursuit of Love* who used to stand, pocket watch in hand, saying: 'If this chap's not here in five minutes, he'll be late'.

People who drive others frantic, because they are so laid back, will probably have *their* reminder of a deadline a long way away from them, and so they feel no pressure to get on with things.

Timelines are endlessly fascinating and ingenious. Ask your friends about theirs: discover how they remember birthdays, the dates of important events; and anything else that you might find useful for yourself.

One of the most important questions is: where do you keep the present: the Now? Create the place and shape of your Now with your hands. Whereabouts is Now in relation to you? Or whereabouts are you in relation to it? And how big a space is Now? Are you right inside that space, or do you spend your life rushing towards the future, or waiting in the past?

Is Now where you would like it to be? What would happen if you experimented with your Now space and made it bigger and more expansive? When Richard Bandler runs seminars, he expands his space to the size of the room, as though everyone in the room has been invited into his living room - they are all welcome guests, and it makes me feel like family.

Expanding and Contracting Time

'Doesn't time fly...'

If we stop to think about it, we realise that for the moments when we are in the here and now - completely absorbed in what we are doing - time does not exist; and, when that moment is gone, we realise that 'time' passed like a flash.

There are also moments when time seems to slow right down, for example when we need to get ourselves out of trouble. My brother tells a tale of running out of road, flying through the air in his car, and taking the key out of the ignition and putting it in his pocket. He had no sense of rush, or panic - just plenty of time to do what he needed to do.

The moment that I use to recapture the stretching of time is when riding a retired racehorse, who liked to take all his fences at a flat-out gallop. He once took a fence with his knees; and, as he went down onto his nose, and I was on the buckle (ie, on the far end of the reins with no contact with his mouth at all), I had all the time in the world to gather him up and keep us both off the floor. Then we galloped on to the next fence, as though nothing untoward had happened.

If we think about these moments, and compare them with more ordinary moments in our lives, we become aware that it is only when our conscious mind kicks in to a 'here and now' moment that we remember the existence of time.

When I was very young, I had a theory that, if I could remember to keep glancing at my watch while I was having a wonderful time, then that wonderful time would last at least ten times as long. But somehow I never remembered to do it.

Learning African Dance with Titos Sompa, one day, I could not get the hang of a sequence of steps: there were too many of them, and it was all too fast. Titos is the most beautiful dancer and a wonderful teacher, so this state of affairs was a first for me, and I realised that it must have something to do with my internal state: I was *trying* - instead of just letting it happen. 'Trance time!', I thought to myself, and allowed my eyes to defocus, my jaw to relax and my tongue to spread and fill my mouth (when you do this, you will discover that your internal voices leave you in peace). Because the jaw muscles are the strongest muscles we have, once I had relaxed my jaw, the rest of my body followed suit, and I soon found myself wondering why we were dancing so *slowly*.

Making Time Work for Us

Tere was feeling overwhelmed by time, combining running a house, ferrying two children to different schools on opposite sides of town, what her husband expected her to do to help him with his work, and her own work. Then she remembered that time was, in fact, her friend: she had planned exactly when she was going to marry, and when she was going to have children - first a girl and then a boy. And so, at precisely the right moment, Armando (now her husband) appeared in her life and everything had gone exactly to plan. Having rediscovered this, she was able to use time *her* way, for a change, again.

Think of all those occasions when you have had a mass of things to do, looked at your watch when you had finished, and discovered that you had achieved them all in apparently no time at all; and then you can play around with expanding and contracting time. How do *you* do it? As Richard Bandler says, who wants to spend what seems like hours standing in a queue, or what seems like days on a transatlantic flight, if you can arrange for the time to pass like a flash?

The important thing to remember about time is that it is yours - to do what you want with.

Come, and Be, with Me

'Disappointment requires adequate planning'
- the unplanned 'now' is the deepest joy.

Time is just a measuring device
- man made;
And we can use it how we will
- as warriors living each day as if it were our last.
So you can come with me
- and be.

Being, there, in the moment
- which is eternity:
Timelessly lost in the sharing of a delicious experience
- an aubergine flower melting in the mouth;
A piano concerto we had not planned
- to enjoy;
The smell of the streets of London

- after long-awaited rain;
The beauty of shape, colour, form and balance
- transporting us to a different plane of being;
The fascination of new connections
- stretching our mind and our imagination.

This just is.

We could step out and look
- forwards, backwards, sideways,
And know that this always was
- and always will be.

Happy in the paradox of the ever-changing
- unchangeable;
Happy in the paradox of now
- and eternity;
Happy in the paradox of individuality
- and belonging to the whole;
Happy in not needing
- to understand,
We may even weep at the beauty of the moment
- if we have time.

Connected, through every cell in our bodies
- to everything that is, has been and will be,
We vibrate in totality in the here and now
- and our joy can only spread throughout the universe.

You may be used to watching clocks
- and giving yourself a hard time.

Yet know that there are always choices
- always different models of the universe.

You can choose your own dance
- and be kind to yourself.

If you choose to be
- you can come with me.

You, Me and Us: Relationships

The Universe sent us Jemma, also known as Flabbergast, or even - sometimes - 'the Ghastly Flabber': just as we were beginning to think that we knew quite a lot about dogs, along came this unruly flatcoated retriever puppy who was a complete law unto herself, and quite unlike any flatcoat we had ever known. Jemma was definitely a challenge to our flexibility, and we often had to admit that we were flummoxed. Frequently, all we knew about what was going on was that whatever we were doing was not working, and that it was therefore time to try something different.

We had to learn to live together in a way that would suit us all: we had to learn about Jemma, and Jemma had to learn about us. We expected certain behaviours from her and she expected certain behaviours from us; and the most important thing about the whole issue was to maintain the relationship - not necessarily easy when this enormous, powerful dog was leaping up at our visitors, with her teeth at face height.

Jemma is not into half measures: in her model of the world, every single human is a passionate dog lover - she has no evidence to the contrary. Her positive intention is to welcome these dog lovers, and to commit herself totally to demonstrating her utter pleasure and delight at their presence.

People kiss their nearest and dearest and Jemma's mouth is just as important to her as a means of demonstrating love: one of her ways of expressing total devotion is to sink her teeth into whatever part of the loved one is nearest to her; this could be your wrist, as you are stroking her or - as in my son Mark's case - the sleeve of a brand new sweater (while he was reading, and noticing with surprise that - for once - there were no teeth in his arm).

I hate darning, but one must occasionally do things that one dislikes.

As you might imagine, the response that Jemma gets does not always correspond to the meaning of her communication - particularly if one of our visitors has had a bad experience with a dog in the past. While we were well aware of the positive intention, we could not accept the behaviour; and so we resorted to the rolled-up newspaper, which makes an alarming noise when applied (even to the side of one's own leg), but does not actually hurt; and now, once we start deliberately rolling newspapers, Jemma changes her behaviour: in other words, all four feet stay on the ground - at least for as long as she can stand the restraint.

Jemma is unique and completely enchanting. We love her dearly and would only want behaviours that are uniquely her own; therefore, the last thing we would want to do would be to exert 'power' to force unnatural behaviour upon her.

At the French Cavalry School in Saumur, the world famous *Cadre Noir*, who are the epitome of elegance in their black uniforms, can be seen performing the *Reprise des Sauteurs*: this is a musical demonstration of old military manoeuvres - using the natural movements of the horse to get you out of trouble when surrounded by foot soldiers.

There is the *Courbette*, when the horse rears: as a self-respecting foot soldier, you would move pretty fast when confronted by a huge and powerful horse towering over you on its hind legs and looking as though it were going to descend upon you at any moment. There is the *Croupade*, when the horse kicks out with both hind legs - a guaranteed scatterer of any threat from behind. Both these movements are natural behaviour to a horse. The third, and most spectacular, movement is the *Cabriole*, when the horse leaps up into the air and then kicks out behind - and you can watch young horses, bursting with energy, doing this when they are playing and having fun.

The point of this digression is that the *Cadre Noir* would never dream of teaching a horse to produce an unnatural behaviour: (a) this would debase his dignity and (b) he would not enjoy it. And the same thing applies with people; we would not want to force our nearest and dearest into a behaviour just to please us - it would not be genuine unless it were natural for them.

*****

If we can apply the principle of positive intentions to other people's behaviour, it makes life a lot simpler. And, if we can also tell the other person what effect their behaviour is having upon us - while acknowledging and honouring the positive intention - it makes life simpler still. And I think that the trick here is to be flexible enough to find an equivalent of the rolled-up newspaper: a way that will get the other person's attention, but will not hurt - and, if the behaviour continues nonetheless, roll up the newspaper again: this is the same principle as my husband's use of: 'I thought we had come to an arrangement whereby.........' which we discussed earlier.

On Telling the Truth

I am a serious believer in telling the truth and, by 'the truth' I mean whatever is true to us at the time; otherwise:

(a) how can other people discover what we need from any relationship?

(b) how can anyone else know what we are experiencing as a result of what they are doing?

(As a sweeping generalisation, it would seem that this sort of telling the truth is often easier for women than it is for men. Women seem to like talking anyway - their roles have programmed them as family communicators and peacemakers, whereas men have been brought up to be 'strong', and this may include not displaying their emotions, and keeping their problems to themselves.)

Relationships change over time and I believe that, when we find ourselves griping about our partner, it is often worth going back to the beginning and asking ourselves what was important to us about this person in the first place.

What was it that we originally found so wonderful about this man or woman?

- If the attraction was that he was 'strong and silent', then the fact that that he does not talk much now cannot really come as much of a surprise.

- If she was always so beautifully turned out, then the fact that she takes hours to get ready to go anywhere does not necessarily signify any great change.

Love is a curious, fascinating thing, and it's worth asking ourselves how and why we fell into it. There will probably be lots of reasons, and the things that we are griping about now will be behaviours, rather than the person's identity: what they are doing, rather than who they are; so it is interesting to make a list of those behaviours that we found irresistible in the first place, and then to ask ourselves whether those behaviours are being maintained, and whether it is these behaviours that are now driving us mad.

For example:

Reasons for attraction	Reasons for gripes
Takes control of the situation	Tries to control me
Enjoys my cooking	Eats too much
So laid back	Has no idea of time
Gets on well with my family	Sides with my family
Wide range of interests	Spends too much time on hobbies
Good talker	Never stops talking

and so on

The American Psychologist, Stephen Gilligan, has the habit of dropping little bombshells which revolutionise my life; and the irritating thing about these bombshells is that they are so obvious, and I could have worked them out for myself, if I had bothered to stop and think. The first one, which I have quoted endlessly ever since, went something like this:

Life, in itself, is utterly meaningless: it just is.

It is the interpretation that we put upon it which decides whether we make ourselves miserable or enjoy ourselves.

I was gob-smacked - to use the technical term. Of course! I knew that! I just didn't know that I knew it, until that moment.

I was sliding into a delicious trance one day - the way one does, when one is with Stephen - when he dropped another bombshell, this time about relationships:

The other person in our relationship is not, and can never be, part of us: because HE OR SHE IS ANOTHER PERSON.

What is part of us is the relationship.

Of course! Why had I never thought that through? Not only is it so blindingly obvious, it also gives us a solid basis from which to ask ourselves some sensible questions.

- Do I want to maintain this relationship?

- If I maintain it, what will that give me?
- If I maintain it, what will I lose?
- If I don't maintain it, what will that give me?
- If I don't maintain it, what will I lose?
- What is it about the relationship that is so important to me?
- What do I need to do?

And, as always, we need to keep on asking the 'what will that give me?' question, until we are high enough up the logical levels to be sure that this is what we really want.

Remembering Stephen's injunction that the other person is someone else, there are two sets of questions that can be usefully asked about any relationship:

What do I want, for me?   *What do you want, for you?*

What do I want for you?   *What do you want for me?*

What do I want for both of us?   *What do you want for both of us?*

What do we both want for both of us?

And the follow-on to all these questions is: 'How will you know when you've got it?' What will your evidence be?

If you want a new car, your evidence could be that you are holding the log book, with your name on it, in your hand; but, if you want a nominalisation like 'love' (which you cannot put in a wheelbarrow), how will you know when you've got it? Will your beloved put your slippers out for you? Or buy you flowers? Or bring you breakfast in bed? Or look at you in a special way? Or speak to you in a certain tone of voice? Or give you lots of cuddles? *What is your evidence that somebody loves you?* Not only do you need to know, your beloved needs to know too, so that he or she can provide that evidence for you.

A cautionary tale that I tell endlessly is about a couple who loved each other dearly but yet felt that their marriage was falling apart. I asked her how she knew that he loved her: 'Because of the melting look he gives me', came her reply - without hesitation. I then asked him the same question: 'Because of the tone of her voice', he answered at once.

Neither of them paused for a instant: their answers came straight from their unconscious minds. She *knew* that melting looks were the only proof of love; he *knew* that a certain tone of voice was the only proof of love - neither of them had any doubt that their evidence was the only evidence there could possibly be. And so, loving each other to bits, she gave him loving, melting looks - but he *heard* none of the evidence that he needed; and he spoke to her in loving tones - but she *saw* none of the evidence that she needed.

The other thing to be aware of is that your replies to these questions need not be graven in stone; we change, and grow, so we can allow ourselves to update our answers at any time - as new, and even more exciting ideas come to us. Thinking about changes in relationships, an interesting and fun thing to do *for your self* is to go back in time once again and call in some outside wisdom, by reminding yourself of what you used to love by way of books, plays, music, poetry, art and so on; and then to ask yourself whether these still remain favourites; in other words, which beliefs and values that attracted you to your favourite works have stood the test of time, and your own changes? And how and why have they managed to stand the test of time?

For example: Noel Coward and Oscar Wilde still delight me as much as, if not more than, ever; because I believe that, if you have something important to say, that it is more effective to get your message across through humour than by making a seriously important speech; and Coward and Wilde were masters of precision with words. Wilde has been described as the prince of paradox, and accepting and enjoying paradox is another way to simplify one's life. Ella Fitzgerald and Billie Holiday encouraged, and are still encouraging, generations of incurable romantics, through the combinations of the words and the music that they chose to sing; like Dr Pangloss in *Candide*, I choose to believe that all is for the best, in the best of all possible worlds, so I will never tire of these two jazz ladies.

Although none of my family ever learned to play a musical instrument, I was brought up on Gilbert and Sullivan, who delight me to this day. And so, when a friend introduced me to opera years later, I already had a passion for operetta and theatre as a foundation for appreciation of this new experience. The basis for the joy I get from opera is the combination of what I experience as a result of what I see on the stage, and hear in a combination of words and music, which engage both my conscious and my unconscious: it is the whole package - a totality of man's endeavour in art and music (both the grand idea and the precision of its realisation) - which satisfies my belief that the whole is so infinitely greater than the sum of its parts.

It's interesting to read, listen to and look at old favourites again, and discover what leaps out and grabs our attention this time. Our filters change according to what we are looking for. For example, if I believe that you do not appreciate my cooking, every time you refuse a second helping, I will interpret that as further proof of my belief. Alternatively, if I believe that you are overweight, every time you refuse a second helping, my interpretation will be that you are paying attention to my admonitions.

Art, literature and music all tap into our unconscious minds: into the beliefs and values that may be so deeply hidden that we may be unaware of them at a conscious level. It might also be interesting to think about what you do not like, in the way of art, music and literature, and to ask yourself what it is about them that you don't like. Saying: '*I just don't*' is not a suitable answer for NLP-ers: you will automatically get the question: 'how do you know?'

- What do you see in your mind's eye?
- What do you hear in your mind's ear?
- What do you feel?
- What do you taste?
- What do you smell?
- What is it that happens inside you that produces the knowledge that you don't like something?

And how have your tastes changed over time? The answers to these questions will tell you a lot about yourself. For example, I used to hate Mozart because he was so predictable; I now love him because he is so balanced. However, although my life is much more balanced these days, I would still prefer to watch an unpredictably brilliant tennis player than an automaton; the reason I watch tennis is in order to be stimulated and inspired by heights of unusual brilliance, and so I find watching someone who plays like a machine completely boring - however good he or she may be.

I hadn't seen Noel Coward's *Private Lives* for about thirty years, and I was fascinated to discover all the things that I had missed or forgotten from the first time around. The divorced Elliot and Amanda find themselves on adjoining balconies in the South of France, each of them on their second honeymoon; the atmosphere takes on the celebrated Coward brittleness, as they discuss their new spouses with one other, and the differences in their new marriages from the stormy, passionately-involved relationship they had had with each other. Their new marriages are very nice, very calm and very dull, and they have to decide what they want from a relationship: do they want niceness and calm? Or do they want storm, passion and involvement? While they are discussing this, they realise that they need to invent their version of the rolled-up newspaper to bring the discussion back to earth, when storm and passion are overtaking them.

Thirty years on, I found even more to delight and entrance me and, more importantly, to make me think. *Private Lives* has definitely stood the test of time for me; and the question is why? This experiment is an excellent way of getting brain and body working as one system, because you will be experiencing your own emotions as a result of other people's thoughts. Not only will you enjoy it, you will learn a lot about yourself, and about all those things that you hold dear.

And, as you reflect upon a relationship, you can also be aware of what the universe sends along to help you to think things through; in other words, what seems to pop into your consciousness from outside, at just the right moment? It could be a picture that catches your eye; it could be something you hear on the radio; it could be something you read; it could be something a friend says; it could be anything. For example, while I was writing about spiders, in the section about flexibility, I went to make a cup of tea and met, wandering across the kitchen floor, a breed of spider I had never seen before.

While we are concentrating consciously upon one thing, our unconscious is processing a million and one thoughts in the background and preparing us to receive all the outside wisdom that is on offer. For example, how often has someone said: 'I've never forgotten what you said about....' - when you have no recollection of saying any such thing. Some passing remark that you made just happened to fit in with whatever that person was processing at that moment. Pearls of wisdom seem to come at us out of the blue, just when we need them; we can call this 'luck', or we can quote Einstein's theory that coincidence is just God's way of remaining anonymous.

Emotions Prove that You are Alive

If we have been educated that everything must be logical, factual and explainable, then the likelihood is that we will not allow ourselves to pay attention to our emotions. Have you ever asked a child (or were you ever asked yourself) 'why did you do that?' and got an infuriating 'I don't know' - or even silence - as an answer? This was because the child could not come up with a reply that would be 'rational' enough to satisfy you. How many average grown-ups do you know who would be satisfied with: 'I had this feeling'; 'I saw this red blur'; 'this voice said I couldn't do it, and I had to show that I could'?

Because our emotions do not seem to be explainable in a logical way, we assume from an early age that we are not supposed to have them; and we may well also assume that, because they are so unacceptable, we are the only people who do have them. We may even go as far as deciding that having emotions is bad, and adopt all the guilt that goes with being bad.

The inevitable outcome of all this is that we repress the emotions which we are quite entitled to experience - they are a part of us, they show that we are alive; and, if we repress them, they are going to try other ways of expressing their needs - sometimes to the extent of making us ill, in order to ensure that they get what they want for us which, as we know, is nothing but the best.

Anger

A client came to see me about the anger, which she felt was eating her up. She had had an affair which had ended badly and was now in the grip of an all-consuming rage against her ex-lover - 'which I know I shouldn't be', she said, struggling between the pain and the guilt. We found out what the pain wanted for her - it wasn't anger at all, it just wanted her to feel okay about her*self*, despite what had happened.

About a year later she rang to tell me that the universe had arranged for her to meet him again - in the most unlikely of places; they had both laughed, and hugged each other, and she felt 'really good about it all'.

Confusion

I believe that one of the biggest stumbling blocks in relationships is confusion. We are rather inclined to measure other people's behaviour against our own (which is perfectly reasonable, as our own can be a useful template), and to become confused when the other person does not behave in a way that we would expect, according to our measurement.

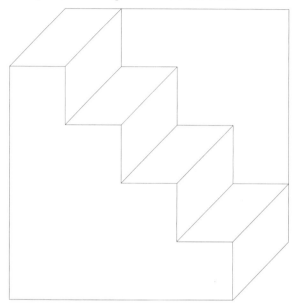

Schröder's Staircase

To illustrate the brain's need to understand, look at this picture. Are these four steps on the ground inside the room, or are you seeing the underside of a staircase which is above your head? If you look at the picture for a bit, with relaxed eyes, you will discover that the stairs appear to move. Your brain likes to understand, in order to make a decision and, in this instance, it has not got enough information to make a decision; so it will go on searching, checking out the possibilities, in the hope of getting more information.

Confusion has curious effects on people. John Grinder once gave us all the task of taking on different states - decided by him - and mine was 'confusion'. At the same time, we had to go round and talk to other people, and guess what states they had adopted. People seemed to be confused by mine (which, I suppose, was hardly surprising) and so, to give them a hint, I remember shouting across the room: 'John! What the hell is going on?'. Later, he said, gently: 'It was interesting to notice how aggressive you became in confusion'. I was surprised: of course I wasn't being aggressive!

I was just playing the part I'd been given; and John, being John, left it at that, knowing that I would work it out for myself, when the time was right. On later reflection, of course, I realised there were dozens of other ways I could have chosen to give the hint, but I'd chosen an aggressive one because that was how I was feeling.

If someone is behaving in a way that we find ridiculous, hurtful, childish - you name it - and we cannot understand why, we are likely to become confused, and to take on all the behaviours that go with our state of confusion. My father, who was absolutely charming to people he understood, used to be unbelievably rude to people who did not agree with the beauty/efficiency/practicality of his ideas; and it is only now that I realise that this was because he could not understand how anybody could fail to appreciate the rightness of what he proposed.

So how do you react to confusion? Just pretend, for a moment, that you are confused and discover what happens inside you. What happens to your internal pictures, sounds and feelings? And how are you likely to react to what is going on inside you?

When you have discovered what happens, stand up, shake it all off and think about the last time you laughed so much that your face hurt (this is a very useful trick for bringing yourself out of an uncomfortable state).

In *Lazy Learning*, there is a horribly confusing intelligence test, and I have had lots of feedback from readers; for example, Patryzia told me that she suddenly found herself four pages further on, without having taken in a single word; Jesper simply said to himself: 'Why would I want to do this test? I do not know anything about the subject', and skipped it. When I first did the test, I got a horrible burbling noise in my ears and all my learning channels promptly closed down.

If someone's behaviour is confusing you, just being aware that you are confused will alleviate the symptoms.

*****

The thing to remember about relationships is that they too are systems. Whatever you do is going to affect the relationship as much as whatever your partner does. It takes two to tango, and one of the most useful techniques you can use if you are having difficulty in understanding what is going on in any relationship - be it at work or at play - is the Meta Mirror, which we did on 19. This will take you outside the system, and give you a far better understanding of what is going on; why the other person is behaving in a particularly way; and why you are behaving in the way you are behaving.

And, having discovered what is going on, you can make the necessary adjustments to your internal state.

We cannot change other people - what we can do is change ourselves, and everything else will follow on from that.

Our Relationship with Ourselves

'But how shall we expect charity towards others, when we are uncharitable to ourselves? Charity begins at home, is the voice of the world; yet is every man his greatest enemy, and, as it were, his own executioner.' - Sir Thomas Browne 1605 - 1682.

One of my most firmly-held beliefs is that the basis of all good relationships is the one that we have with ourselves. If we feel safe and comfortable with ourselves, then we can take this safe, comfortable state into any other relationship - with the result that the other person will feel safe and comfortable with us.

As a linguist, I have a passion for the origins and derivations of words and phrases and so, for the origin of 'self-confidence', I turn to my Latin dictionary:

'Confidere: to trust, have faith in, rely upon, believe, be assured'
- which, I think, when referring to oneself, just about says it all.

Working with a young client (who could possibly be described as arrogant - but I knew better), I asked him what would happen if he felt okay about himself. There was a long, warming pause as he tried this idea on for size: his skin colour changed, his body settled, relaxed and expanded within itself, the contours of his face softened and, although I can't consciously see auras, all his lights went up. Eventually, calm, smiling and sparkling with life he said: 'Great!'. I then asked what could possibly stop him from feeling okay about himself in the future, and all the old conditioning and programming came back: 'I'm not perfect' was the instant response. 'Who is?', I asked. 'Jesus was!', he replied, and this appeared to clinch the argument as far as he was concerned.

We had already talked about separating the different logical levels, in order to keep our thinking from getting into a serious muddle, and so I said that I thought that ideas about the perfection of Jesus were largely based upon his behaviours; whereas what we were talking about now was identity. Our behaviours and mistakes were all things that we could learn from, whereas our identity is unique: we are who we are, and how we behave is a different matter altogether.

The most important thing about you is that *you are you, and there is no one else like you in the whole world*. And that self of yours has been looking after you every minute, of every hour, of every day - from the moment you were born. The proof that it has done a good job is that you have survived in this complicated, often dangerous world. And that is something you can feel really good about.

There is a lovely poem by Virginia Satir, the American family therapist, called *Self Esteem* (see the Bibliography) and, when I have foreign students here, the first thing we do is to read it and make sure they have understood it; then they illustrate it for themselves. The recurring theme throughout this poem is: '*I am me. And I am okay*'.

So take a little time for yourself, for a change.

Switch off the doorbell, shove the telephone in the 'fridge, put on some of your favourite music, settle yourself somewhere warm and comfortable with 'DO NOT DISTURB' on the door, and just indulge yourself in thinking about all those different parts of you that work so hard on your behalf - every minute, of every hour, of every day: you are going to create the ambience for a meeting of all those different parts of you; a meeting where they can get together and get to know, and appreciate each other.

For a start, you can call in your self-indulgence part to give you some moral support when your 'this is a shocking waste of time' part starts to object - because spending this time on yourself will be worth more than pure gold for you.

Then you can call in your kindness part, your appreciative part, your TLC (tender, loving care) part, your host part - and any other part of you that you need - to make this an enjoyable, valuable gathering. As each of them arrives, give them a big hug, and lots of thanks and appreciation; make sure that they all know and appreciate each other and then tell them what you want to do, and why - and ask for their help and suggestions about who else needs to be invited to this great gathering, in order to give you all moral support at this most valuable of meetings.

The magic trick here is to get together as many of those different parts of you as possible, so that they can get to know and appreciate each other, and to value each other's contribution to the enterprise that is you. As there may be parts of you who seem completely opposed to each other, the important thing about the moral support team is the warm, welcoming atmosphere that they create, so that everyone feels honoured, appreciated, comfortable, safe and secure.

When the guaranteed support team is there, you can then start to invite other parts of you that you need to talk to - and there may be several that you were completely unaware of at a conscious level.

Some suggested guests (I have called these parts by their functions, or what they say - you might prefer to give them names):

- Giving yourself a hard time
- Laziness
- 'This is a load of rubbish'
- 'I don't want to succeed'
- 'I am hopeless'
- 'If I don't try, I can't fail'
- 'What makes you think you're important?'
- 'I can't do this'
- The organiser

I am sure you will be able to think up some more. And remember:

ALL THESE PARTS OF YOU HAVE POSITIVE INTENTIONS - they all want nothing but the best for you: that is their job.

Allow yourself to relax deep inside yourself as you communicate with all these different parts of you - from the top of your head, to the tip of your nose, to the tips of your fingers and the tips of your toes.

Allow your thoughts to wander, and observe what pictures flash up in your mind's eye; these pictures will be communications from yourself to you and you can take as long as you like to explore and enjoy them.

If there is a picture that you do not understand, all you need to do is to say that you do not understand, and ask that part of you to send you something that will be clear to you: pictures that will make sense to you; or maybe words instead of pictures - whatever would be right for you.

And while you are becoming more and more aware of the pictures that come into your mind's eye, you can listen to the sounds that come into your mind's ear: these are more communications. Your self will be so delighted that you are, at last, paying attention that it will be bubbling with information to surprise and delight you.

And, as all this is happening, you may feel that your body would like to readjust itself to incorporate all this new information; you can allow it to do whatever it needs to do in order to make itself more and more comfortable, and at ease with itself. And, as you are doing this, you can become aware of all the feelings and movements within you.

Maybe there are micro-twitches corresponding to readjustments in your neurology, maybe your stomach is starting to rumble, as your thoughts flow through you more and more freely; maybe there is a twitch in your left, big toe to remind you that it has a message for you. What are all these messages about? Ask them.

And, as the parts of you that may not always seem too easy to live with start to arrive, you can welcome them with ease, comfort and pleasure. When your 'giving myself a hard time' part arrives, you can ask it what it wants for you. It probably simply wants you to succeed; and it will be delighted to notice that you are succeeding in communicating with it, as well as with all your other parts. As a good host, you will naturally want to introduce to each other all the other parts of you that want you to succeed: they will have so much in common that they will happily make friends, enjoy themselves and negotiate together on your behalf - to achieve the success that they want, in the best possible way for you.

And, as a superb host or hostess, you will want to ensure that all your parts meet others who share their interests and dreams for you, so that they can get to know each other at a really deep level - because they will want to be able to work together on your behalf, to create that future that they and you want for yourself.

And this may be such a relaxing occasion that you may drift down deeper, and deeper into enjoyment and appreciation of everything that is going on; of everything that each part of you is doing for you; of how much you and they value each other, and you may even go to sleep, and - knowing, at the deepest level, the whole is infinitely greater than the sum of its parts - allow all those parts of you to organise themselves, so that they can work together to achieve all your dreams - and more - without any interference from you.

You can do whatever you would like to do, and enjoy it all at the deepest level.

Whatever you choose to do, you can allow yourself as much time as you need; and, when you finally decide that it is time to do something different, you will know that all those parts of you can continue to process everything that they and you have discovered, even though *you* may be occupied with something completely different.

And I don't know what wonderful things you will discover about yourself, as you explore; all I do know is that, when you choose to come back to the here and now you will feel alert, refreshed and delighted with your new knowledge; and with the knowledge that, the more often you relax in this way, and communicate with yourself, the more joyful your life will become.

You might like to record all this on tape - over a piece of relaxing music (preferably baroque or Mozart); speaking in just the soft, gentle voice that you would like to hear, allowing your words to flow with the music, and leaving plenty of pauses for you to process the suggestions and enjoy your self.

Man's Best Friend

Once upon a time, in a faraway land, there lived a poor, sad lonely man. He was lonely because he did not understand about friendship: he did not know the warmth, comfort and pleasure that comes from friendship; and, because he did not know that such delights existed, he had never thought about how to make friends; and, because he had never thought about how to make friends, he had never learned how to do it.

He lived alone in the forest, as far away from other people as he could get. He did not trust other people. Other people were strangers - he did not know them, and he did not trust the unknown. The unknown was unpredictable: you did not know how it would behave; you could not rely upon the unknown. The unknown was dangerous.

From time to time, when his supplies ran out, he would have to go to the nearest town. Everyone in the town knew who he was: he was 'poor Ben' - the strange man who lived alone in the forest; the nervous man who would hardly acknowledge their greetings; the man who looked away when you talked to him. They felt sorry for him, and wished he were happier: they knew the joys of friendship; they knew that this man was just another human being who needed to be connected to the rest of the world; but, because Ben was so distrustful of strangers, he would allow no one's friendly greeting to get through to his heart.

And eventually, when their greetings did not work, the townspeople began to resent him: they were hurt by being rejected, and so they tried some different ways of communicating with him. They tried ignoring him; they tried calling him names; they tried to bully him into talking to them - but nothing worked: Ben remained isolated, by himself, in his shell, protected from all outside influence: protected from anything and everything that might change his life, protected from love, from warmth, from friendship and from belonging.

And then, one day, a strange thing happened. Ben was sitting in the town square, waiting for his supplies to be made up, when a beautiful dog came and sat down beside him, put a gentle paw onto his knee and gazed adoringly into his eyes. Ben looked at this interloper into his silence, and wondered. He wondered how it was that there was someone else in his space, and realised that it did not feel like an invasion; he wondered why this dog was giving him his trust; and he wondered at his pleasure and delight at the encounter.

And I don't know how long man and dog sat there and communicated with one another; all I do know is that Ben had not noticed that the dog was on a lead and that, at the end of the lead, there stood a tall, smiling young man who watched and waited while the two of them enjoyed each other's company.

Eventually, the young man spoke.

'Good day to you', he said. 'My name is Adam, and this is Ben.' Our friend looked up at him, in surprise. 'The dog's name is Ben', the young man repeated, smiling. 'And he's looking for a new master because I've got to go away and live in the big city, which I know he'll hate because he's a country dog.'

Ben Dog gave Ben Man's hand a lick, and gazed up at him again. Ben Man looked down at the dog's paw resting in his hand and thought: 'Funny. You see people hand in hand, but I haven't held hands with anybody since I was a child. And it's rather nice.' He smiled up at the young man, and realised that he had not smiled at anybody for years, either - and that that felt rather nice too.

'The only trouble is,' the young man went on, musingly 'that he's been known to chase sheep, so he needs to live somewhere where there are no sheep.' Ben Man thought about his little house deep in the forest, and of how the only farm animals on his way to the town were cows, and that cows were not afraid of dogs. He nodded, and went on looking at the dog.

He was very beautiful, and very elegant: big, black and powerful with a thick shining coat; his hind legs were so well feathered that he looked as though he were wearing trousers, and he had a thickly feathered tail. But the most beautiful thing about him was his head: his long nose swept up to a domed forehead, around wide-set, almond-shaped eyes which gave him an open, honest appearance. Looking at him, you felt that you could trust him, as a faithful friend.

'I wonder, Ben', said the young man quietly, squatting down beside the dog 'what your new friend's name is.' The dog gave his face a quick lick, and then gave his new friend's hand a lick too, for good measure.

Ben Man looked down at Adam. What a nice, open face he had; what a nice, gentle, relaxed manner. There seemed to be warmth emanating from him: it almost seemed as if he had light dancing round him. Ben felt comfortable with this man. If only everyone else in the world were like him. This man was no threat, he was just easy to be with.

'Well, funnily enough, my name's Ben too', he said. The dog wagged his tail at the mention of his name, and then rested his chin on our friend's knee. Ben stroked the domed head and felt soothed by the rhythm of the strokes, by the warmth of the dog and by the connection with another living creature. 'Strange!' he thought to himself, 'it feels as if the three of us are here, in our own private world'; he looked around, '... and yet, the rest of the world looks brighter.'

He noticed the passers-by looking at the group and smiling; he knew them all by sight, and he smiled back - surprised at how good all this made him feel.

He noticed that the sun was shining, that the fountain was playing, that the birds were singing, that the delivery boys where whistling; he noticed the bright colours, the bustle in the market place, the market vendors' cries, the smells from the bakery, the smells from the coffee shop, the groups of people in their own world, and yet part of his world. People smilingly bade them good day, in passing, and Ben smiled and returned their greeting. People stopped to admire the dog - a dog is always an excuse for conversation - and Ben Dog returned their admiration with wagging and pleasure. Children came up to talk. 'It's funny,' thought Ben, 'I've never liked children before, but these ones are charming: they're so interesting and such fun.'

And so the morning went by at its own pace. Ben and Adam talked about this and that, or sat in companionable silence while Ben allowed himself to become aware of the differences he was discovering in this same old world which seemed entirely new.

And later they walked along the river together, while Ben Dog leapt in and out of the water, chased water weed, or galloped along the bank in his enjoyment at the expending of energy. He was fast, and wonderful to watch as he galloped, and the combination of energy, elegance, power and beauty entranced Ben Man; he felt he could watch him all day.

The sun danced off the river as it flowed past the overhanging willows; dragonflies whirred in and out of their vision, the ducks busied themselves with their affairs, the moorhens argued with each other, the smell of the meadowsweet wafted into their nostrils and a skylark sang overhead. It was a good day to be alive. And, at the end of this perfect day, Ben Dog went home with Ben Man - to his new life in the forest.

*****

Ben Man adored his new companion, and the feeling was mutual. He lavished every care upon him and, as time went by, Ben Dog got fatter and fatter, and Ben Man got thinner and thinner. He would feed Ben Dog nothing but the best, which meant that he could not afford to feed himself properly. The other problem was that Ben Dog was always kept on a lead.

One day, as they were walking through the forest together, they met a gentle old man whom they had never seen before. Ben Dog liked him at once (but then Ben Dog liked everybody). Ben Man liked him too - he reminded him of Adam: he seemed to have that same warm, welcoming, bright comfortable light around him. They talked about the dog, about the weather, about the forest, about this and that, and about the dog again.

'I was wondering,' said the old man, 'why you kept him on the lead'.

'Oh, I have to,' replied Ben, 'otherwise he'd run away'.

'I wonder why he'd do that,' mused the old man, gently. Ben thought for a while, and couldn't come up with an answer.

'Who's his best friend?' the old man asked, after a bit.

'Well... I am... I suppose.'

'And would you run away from your best friend?'

Ben thought some more, and realised that he'd never stopped to ask himself such a perfectly simple question. He smiled, and undid the dog's lead. Ben Dog, after a moment's hesitation, went off to explore all the interesting smells round about.

'You'll find,' said the old man, *'that a dog can do all sorts of things that a man can't do; this is why the man/dog combination is so powerful - why the dog is man's best friend. Notice how his nose and tail work together; when he's found an interesting smell, his tail wags. That's how you'll know what he's discovering.'*

Ben watched his dog in fascination for the rest of the day. The dog always knew where he was as he walked on through the forest; if he ranged too far, he would come back and check that his master was where he thought he was. And, just as Ben Man was beginning to think how hungry he was, and how little there was in the larder, Ben Dog came back proudly with a fine big rabbit, which he deposited at his master's feet.

And so began the true partnership. Ben Man became stronger and healthier, Ben Dog became lithe and streamlined and fit again: and they both experienced the joy and satisfaction of working together as a team, and relying upon and trusting each other.

And it happened that times were getting harder and harder, in the rest of the world, and that everybody had less and less work, and less and less money; and what made things worse was that there was a plague of rabbits who ate all the crops that people tried to grow in order to feed themselves. So the Bens, as everybody in the little town now called them, were able to supply fresh meat for the people who could not afford to buy it. Not only that, but the crops could now grow and increase and multiply, as they had been created to do, and so everyone had plenty to eat.

And, as time went by, the Bens became important and valued members of their community, enjoying the sharing of love, respect, friendship, trust, ideas, co-operation and everything else that goes with life - and all because they had learned to enjoy themselves so completely.

People at Work (and at Play)

Opinion is divided as to what makes the world go round: some say it is money and some say it is love; and, if we take our thinking up to a higher level, we discover that the common denominator of these two apparently disparate theories is people. It is people who want to make money; it is people who want to get together, work together, play together, get to know each other, form relationships and create whatever it is that they want to create together.

Work is supposed to be an objective world: a detached world which can be directed from the outside; a world where, if we apply the right rules, everything will go according to plan; but - as we all know - once people are involved, plans can go awry. NLP has been described as the study of the structure of subjectivity - in other words, it applies objectivity to a world of subjectivity: a world where people's internal states direct their behaviours and, as a result, change the behaviours of the people around them.

The more we try to be objective, the less we may be consciously aware of the effects of subjectivity upon our work. For example, two of the most important exponents of Behaviourism came to dramatically different conclusions about conditioning, as a result of their carefully controlled 'objective' experiments.

The Russian Pavlov proved that all human behaviour is a conditioned reaction, by ringing a bell before he fed his dogs: after he had been doing this for some time, the dogs salivated when they heard the bell - even if Pavlov did not feed them.

The American Skinner proved that behaviour is shaped and maintained by its consequences: in other words, if you're polite to Great Aunt Mary, I'll give you a sweet; or, if you're naughty, Father Christmas won't come.

Although I do not doubt that each of them carried out their work with a meticulous conscientious objectivity, when we compare the way that they set up their experiments, we become aware that Pavlov controlled his in accordance with the conditions prevailing in Russia at the time: *no freedom of choice*; whereas Skinner, with his Western background, presupposed that people had the freedom to choose. In each case, their subjectivity affected the way they set up and monitored their experiments, and thus the results were radically different.

And the moral of this story is that, however meticulous we are about being objective, our own personal models of the world are going to affect everything that we do, in every section of our lives, and every system we that find ourselves part of at the time.

*****

Business is about people, rather than balance sheets: it is the people in the business who create the figures on the balance sheets. As Colin Reeve, the Management Consultant I modelled for '*Lazy Learning*', says - when asked to look at the bottom line: 'If you change the people, you'll change these figures; whereas, if you change these figures, you won't change the people.'

What do I Want? What do You Want? What do We All Want?

Before we come to communication, which is at Behaviour level, we need to decide what we want. Who are we going to be, as a company? Why are we in business? Do we just want to make loads of money? Do we want to create a business that will grow and last? Do we want to provide the world with something useful at an affordable price? Do we want to change the way that people do things? Do we want to make people's lives simpler? Do we want to give our employees a secure future? What do we want? What is our mission as part of this company? And what will that give us? And what will we lose, if we get it? For example, if we get too big, we may lose the personal touch, which was our reason for starting the company in the first place.

Not only do we need clear outcomes for the business, we also need clear outcomes for ourselves, as a part of this mission. If we achieve our company mission, what do we want to achieve for ourselves at the same time? And what will that give us, as individuals? And what will we lose if we get it? For example, maybe we will have to work so hard to make all that lovely money that we will not have the time to enjoy it - which is why we wanted it in the first place.

Whatever answers you come up with, everyone in the company needs to know what this mission is - otherwise, how can they involve themselves in making the dream come true? Imagine what a display team - like the RAF's Red Arrows - would look like, if each pilot did not know the overall pattern down to the last detail. Or, supposing that top management decides that the customers are the people who matter most to the company - and they do not bother to pass this idea on to the telephonists, or the receptionist - or any of the people up at the sharp end, who are actually in touch with the customers?

And then comes the question: what do you, personally, want from your work? You can apply the same principles, and the same questions to both company and personal outcomes.

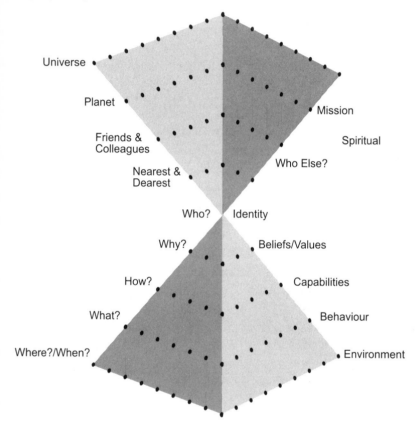

Here is the logical levels diagram again, to save your having to keep referring back to it. You might like to start by asking yourself what you are doing on the planet, and whether you want to fulfil this mission at work or in some other way. Whatever you decide, the best level to go to next is probably Identity, because I believe that, in any system, people need to feel that they matter as people: that they are important for who they are, rather than what they do; that they are part of the overall achievement; that their contribution is important and valued; that their opinions count for something, and so on.

The Australian, Elton Mayo, made some fascinating discoveries in the 1920s at the Hawthorne Works of the Western Electric Company in Chicago. Materially, this company was very progressive: they had a pension scheme, a sickness benefit scheme, recreational facilities and all sorts of other benefits for their workers, but yet there was grumbling and dissatisfaction.

One theory that they tested was that improved lighting improves output. They set up a controlled experiment monitoring two groups: one with improved lighting and one without. The output of the group with improved lighting went up. QED? Maybe; but they noticed with interest that the output of the control group also went up.

The next experiment was with a series of changes to working conditions over a period of five years. They monitored the output of a small group of workers as a result of each change that they made. The original working conditions were: a forty-eight hour week, including Saturdays, and no breaks.

1. They introduced piece work: output went up
2. They introduced two five-minute breaks per day: output went up
3. They increased the breaks to ten minutes: output went up sharply
4. They changed to six five-minute breaks: output went down slightly, and the workers complained that this arrangement interrupted their work rhythm
5. They went back to two breaks, and added a hot meal: output went up
6. They sent the workers home half an hour earlier: output went up
7. They sent the workers home an hour earlier: output remained the same
8. They went back to the original conditions: *output was the highest ever recorded.*

What I deliberately omitted to tell you at the beginning was that, throughout these experiments, there was someone in the workshop all the time, telling the workers exactly what was going on, and why; asking for their help and advice, and listening to their complaints. With this information, the results of the experiments make sense - including the last result which, if we kept our thinking at the environmental level of improvements to working conditions, would be almost impossible to believe. These workers were treated as important people: they were consulted at every turn; it was their group which had been chosen to help the company to solve a problem; they had their own acknowledged place within the company; improvements to the company depended on them; they belonged; they mattered.

If you, too, need to feel valued, the perennial NLP question comes up: *how will you know when you have got it?* What will your evidence be? How will you know that you belong, that you are important, that you matter to your company? What will you see, hear, feel, taste and smell?

- Will the next person up the line tell you, face to face?
- Will the Personnel Manager telephone you once a week?
- Will the Managing Director send you a personal letter?
- Will you get a fax from someone in Head Office?
- Will colleagues give you pats on the back?
- Will you be given a day off?
- Will you get a bonus?
- Will it be because of the way that people look at you?
  the tone of their voice?
  how close they stand to you?

Because we are all different, we all have our own evidence procedures: I once worked with someone who could not believe any compliment that anyone paid her. I asked her what I would have to do in order for her to know that she had done a good job. After a lot of thought, she said the only way she could believe this would be if she overheard me telling someone else that she had done a good job - and she would have to know that I did not know that I was within earshot. What a complicated way to live! This sort of evidence is not easy to find, and consequently she had very little external validation of her work with which to boost her self-esteem.

You could ask your questions about your work in any order of logical levels, for example:

- Planet: what am I doing here? How can I fulfil this role?
- Identity: who do I want to be at work? What title and/or role do I want?
- Beliefs: why do I want to do this particular job/fulfil this role?
- Who else: how will my family be affected by this work identity?
- Who else: how will my colleagues be affected by this identity?
- Capabilities: what do I need to be able to do in order to do this job?
- Behaviours: what will I need to do, to do this job properly?
- Environment: where and when do I want to work?

By asking these questions, you can clarify what you *really* want, so that not only do you know what to aim for, but also there are no surprises - like discovering too late that your family does not care for your travelling six months of the year, or whatever you forgot to take into account when you accepted the job.

Communication

> *"Then you should say what you mean,"* the March Hare went on.
> *"I do,"* Alice hastily replied; *"at least - at least I mean what I say - that's the same thing, you know."*
> *"Not the same thing a bit!"* said the Hatter. *"Why, you might just as well say that* 'I see what I eat' *is the same thing as* 'I eat what I see'*!"*

> - Lewis Carroll: *Alice's Adventures in Wonderland*

Here we are, in our wonderful, modern world, with communication improving by the minute: the Internet - the Information Superhighway, which is supposed to revolutionise our lives - and every technical means you can think of to bring us closer together. And what good does all this do, if we don't communicate with the people closest to home?

Men and women can find themselves locked in mortal combat over gender issues, unable to allow themselves to be aware that they are two sides of the same coin - each with their own way of thinking and being which are vital factors of the whole; parents and teenagers can be entrenched in their own models of the world and unaware that they are just models; workers and bosses can seem to inhabit separate planes - and so on.

For me, effective communication is the foundation stone of almost everything. To work, play and be together successfully, we need to be able to connect with each other, to trust each other, to laugh together.... If we don't communicate, how on earth can we know what is going on? And, if we don't know what is going on, how can we contribute effectively to the system? - Whatever the system may be.

Supposing you have something for me to do. I need to know precisely what you need, and why you need it, in order to come up with the goods. As we discovered earlier, language is a very imprecise medium for communication, not only because words can mean different things to different people, but also because of all the deletion, distortion and generalisation that we do in the course of our communication. If you go back to the section on Language on pages 29 - 34, you will realise that you can use the Meta Model to great effect, in any context. (Michael McMaster and John Grinder have produced an excellent book for business called: *Precision: a New Approach to Communication* - you will find more details in the Bibliography).

In order for me to do this job to your satisfaction, you need to be able to explain to me precisely what you want, in a way that I will understand: maybe words are enough; maybe you need to draw me pictures; maybe you need to walk me through it. It all depends on how I process my thoughts. And I need to be able to ask you precise questions: I need to know exactly what you mean, for example:

• 'quicker than last time'	*- how much quicker than last time?*
• 'a better product'	*- better than what?*
	- better in what way?
• 'not too much over budget'	*- how much over budget is too much?*
• 'quality is important'	*- what aspect of quality is important?*
	- quality is important to whom?
• 'cut the costs'	*- the costs of what? Labour? Advertising?*
	- cut costs by how much?

A week later, you check in to find out how I am getting on. 'Okay', I say. What do I mean by 'Okay'? Am I getting on well with my team? Am I on schedule? Have I at last managed to get the promised supplies from so-and-so? Am I still within the budget? Or am I just trying to get you off my back?

For a start, you will need to know your outcome for asking me the question. Maybe you know that I always produce exactly what you want on time, and that being asked how I am getting on is just part of my evidence procedure that I am important; or maybe this is the first time I have ever done a job for you. What, precisely, do you need to know? And why do you need to know it? And how do you need to ask me the questions in order to get high quality answers - rather than letting me feel that I am being persecuted?

A cautionary tale for you: a student on an NLP Practitioner course had just learned the Meta Model, and decided to practise it (he had somehow got it into his head that brownie points could be scored from every Meta Model infringement - like deletion, distortion or generalisation - that he pounced upon). On the next stage of the course, he proudly described a conversation between himself and a friend, which had gone something like this:

STUDENT: So how was your holiday?

FRIEND: Great!

STUDENT: And how, specifically, was it great?

FRIEND: Well...... the hotel was nice.

STUDENT: And what, specifically, was nice about the hotel?

FRIEND: Um...... well...... the food was good.

STUDENT: And how, specifically, was the food good?

FRIEND: ...... there was...... plenty of....... um....... er....... variety.

STUDENT: In what way, specifically, was there plenty of variety?

FRIEND: For God's sake! Can't one generalise with you at all?

STUDENT: (indignantly) Oh, I'm sorry! I thought you wanted to tell me about your holiday!

And the sad thing is that he thought that he had done a good job. History does not relate whether they are still friends.

As we discovered in 'the meaning of the communication...' rapport is the basis of all successful communication; and, the higher the level at which we can create it, the greater the chances of success. We can go above identity (the 'you matter to me' level) to mission level: if you and I share a passionate commitment to a mission, we will probably be able to put up with each other's behaviour even more easily than we could if our connection was only made at identity level - at least when we were working on our shared mission.

The great thing about higher-level rapport is that it works down the telephone as well. The telephone robs us of all our visual information, so we cannot match or mirror the other person's movements; but, if the person on the other end of the line really matters to you, then that information goes winging down the line with your voice, and he or she will pick it up.

Also, if someone telephones to complain about a mistake your company has made, you are immediately connected at mission level: your customer is upset, and the last thing anyone in your company wants is an upset customer - because, without customers, your company could not exist.

And, while we are on the subject of telephone rapport, a colleague had to ask her staff to stop creating so much rapport on the telephone for outgoing calls, because their telephone bills had suddenly soared: incoming calls were allowed the full treatment.

Listening

The other half of the communication dance is knowing how to listen. At school, they just tell us to listen - presupposing that we know how to do it.

In *Listening - the Forgotten Skill* (see the Bibliography), Madelyn Burley-Allen has produced a fascinating series of questions to help us to evaluate our own listening habits. Not only did it make me stop and think, but also I realised that certain behaviours had simply become habits, and that there were much easier and more effective ways of doing things.

Presupposing that our outcome for listening is to acquire as much information as possible, there are two processes involved:

1. Ensuring that the speaker gives us the information
2. Understanding, coding and filing this information so that we can retrieve it.

In order to give us all the information, the speaker needs to know that he or she has our full attention: have you ever tried to explain something important to someone who did not seem to be remotely interested, or seemed to be in a rush, or whose mind seemed to be somewhere else, or who seemed determined to leap upon and find fault with every small detail - rather than treat what you were saying as a whole?

Because we are all different, evidence of a listener's full attention will vary from speaker to speaker. Some will need eye contact; some will need verbal encouragement, some will need nods, some will need smiles, some will need stillness from us - it all depends on how they process their thinking. So the trick is to do all these things - which is very easy, because all we have to do in order to remember them all is to pretend that we are utterly fascinated by this person, and:

- Look deep into their right eye
- Join them in their model of the world: as if we were there with them
- Or, better still, pretend we are them
- Nod when they nod
- Smile when they smile
- Frown when they frown
- Breathe in when they breathe in
- Laugh when they laugh
- Toss in the odd, appreciative grunt - or whatever seems appropriate

Remember that we were provided with two eyes, two ears and *only one mouth*, and you will discover that your ears simply become open learning channels as all the information pours in; you will find that you will be building up a picture or pictures in your mind's eye and, as more and more information comes in, the gaps in your pictures will fill up; you will be able to recreate the sounds of whatever is being described in your mind's ear; you will pick up the speaker's feelings in your body. In other words, you will be experiencing what the speaker is experiencing, and picking up all sorts of extra information which you would not get if you were not *quietly waiting for the whole message*, rather than leaping in early on with questions which are going to be answered anyway, as the story progresses. We all repeat ourselves in one way or another; and so - if there is something you have not understood the first time - it will be probably be clarified later, in a different way.

When the speaker has finished, you can look at the picture in your mind's eye and, if anything is missing or still not clear, this is when you can ask your questions.

Play around with listening wherever you go, and see what happens: because people are so unused to being listened to properly, they will be delighted to have the chance to really get their message across for once; and, what is more, you will discover that other people can be even more interesting than you expected.

Starting with No 1

'Look after No 1', they say, and in comes the Ministry of Anti-Fun crying:

- SHOCK HORROR!
- Selfishness!
- Ego Trip!
- Love thy neighbour!
- You ought to think of yourself last!
- This awful Me! Me! Me! Society!

And the questions I would ask are:

- If you don't look after your self, who else is going to?
- Who else knows precisely what you need?
- Who else could do the job properly?

So let's stop and think about You for a moment. Let's suppose that you do a lot of travelling, and that the system that you have chosen to get you from place to place is a car: you are going to need to be able to rely on this car absolutely. And, in order to do so, you are going to have to pay attention to the car's needs: for example, you are going to have to give it petrol, oil, water in its windscreen washers, air in its tyres, and so on - otherwise it won't be able to do its job properly. In other words, look after it, and it will look after you.

The same principle applies to your self.

- Look after your self!
- Take care of your self!

Somehow the Ministry of Anti-Fun hasn't yet cottoned on to this wise counsel, which is just as well because, without the co-operation of your self, you will not have the freedom to communicate with others. In other words, if your self feels threatened by A, and cannot rely upon you to support and protect it, up will go the barriers to keep you safe.

I am always quoting Rabbi Lionel Blue (one of my favourite broadcasters), who maintains that 'Love thy neighbour as thyself' means 'as much as thyself'; and therefore, if you do not love yourself, you are of no use whatever to your neighbour. If we stop to think about this for a moment, we will realise that it makes far more sense than putting everyone else first - an instruction which has been deeply inculcated into so many of us, particularly women, in the roles we have been programmed to play.

So stop and think for a moment about your self: that unconscious part of you that has kept you safe for all these years. And say 'hello' to it; and thank it for all that it has done for you; acknowledge and appreciate it. I bet it will be surprised that, at last, you are paying it some attention. You might even like to give it a huge hug, and see what happens.

You can spend as long as you like doing this: being aware at the deepest level that you are unique - that there is no one else like you in the whole world. You might even like to ask your self about Great Aunt Diana's theory that, if the two of you are at ease with each other, then you will suddenly find that you are at ease with everybody else - and see what your self says. You might also ask what would happen if the two of you got together like this on a regular basis, and got to know each other better.

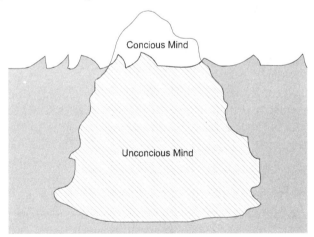

The Tip of the Iceberg

The proportion of conscious to unconscious mind has been described as 'the tip of the iceberg'; if we are going to choose this metaphor, the amount of an iceberg that we can see is probably about one ninth of the total: in other words, we are only consciously aware of one ninth of what is going on inside us.

And so, from a pragmatic point of view, it would seem that - with eight ninths of ourselves acting unconsciously - it is a good idea to have those eight ninths on our side, and co-operating with us.

Criticism or Feedback?

If someone has done something that we cannot condone, we may need to do something about it. And I think that the important question here is: *what is my outcome?* Do I want to make this person feel like a worm? Do I want to release my own frustration? Or do I simply want to ensure that this doesn't happen again?

My dictionary defines 'criticism' as 'the act of judging', and judging pre-supposes that things are either 'right' or 'wrong'; as we have already discovered, our ideas of rightness and wrongness are determined by our individual maps of the world. For example, I like to do things the easy way, whereas there are lots of people who think that if something is too easy, it cannot possibly work. Who is right? And who is wrong? And does it really matter anyway?

If we want to ensure that whatever it is does not happen again, telling people they are idiots is probably not going to achieve our outcome as effectively as we would wish; a discussion, which includes two-way feedback, is far more likely to be successful.

If we presuppose that people do the best they can, according to the information available to them, we have a solid basis from which to discuss what has happened. The easy way to do this is side by side - looking at the problem together: we can either do this sitting down, with the problem out on the table in front of us - maybe drawn on a piece of paper, or using whatever is on the table to represent the different factors, or rerunning an imaginary video of what happened on the opposite wall. Doing it this way separates the person from the problem: it is the problem we are talking about, not the person who was supposedly responsible for it. If people feel that they are being attacked (which they may well do, if we are eyeball to eyeball), they will become defensive, and close up; and, if they close up, we will not get all the information that we need. Whereas, if they feel that we are enlisting their aid, then they will give us all the help that they can in order to solve the problem.

Language Patterns

There are all sorts of ways that we can use language to help, or hinder the situation. Think, for example, of the language that people have used that made you feel defensive. There are words that are almost guaranteed to push people's buttons, like:

- wrong
- should
- ought to
- stupid
- but
- why?

If I launch into telling you that you are wrong, that what you should have done was.... I seem to be setting myself up in a position of superiority, and this presupposes that you are inferior, which is not going to do much for your internal state - or our discussion. The other point about my supposedly knowing better than you is that I probably was not there when it happened and, as we all know, nothing is relevant outside its context; if I was not there, then I am in no position to judge.

If I make identity-level statements, like: *You are* wrong/stupid/irresponsible/arrogant, or whatever, then it is you that we are discussing - rather than the problem in question; it is you who is on the firing line and, once again, this is not going to help the situation.

I need to know *how* the incident happened, rather than why. And 'why' can be a very intrusive word - particularly when accompanied by a pointed finger. 'Why' often seems to be going for the jugular: for our purposes, it is altogether too close to identity level, whereas the 'hows', 'whats', 'wheres' and 'whens' are what we need to know about the problem.

What happens when I phrase things like this:

'I have been very pleased with your work, but.........

'You are a valuable member of our team, but.........

need I say more? If you want to phrase things in this way, what would happen if you substituted 'and' for 'but'?

And, while we are on the subject, I wonder what would happen if you began suggestions to other people with 'I wonder what would happen if........', rather that just telling them what to do. I don't know about you, but I don't like being told what to do; it smacks of being ordered about (my father was a soldier, so I had had enough of being ordered about at a very early age). 'What would happen if you.......?' gives people the choice of doing it or not.

In *The Night* Terence Stamp describes a moment when the hero stops talking to his wife and starts 'telling' her. I am bolshie by nature and so, if you *tell* me what to do, I'll probably do the exact opposite - consciously, or otherwise; and, while I know that this is just me, I also believe that most of us like to feel that (a) we are intelligent enough to be able to evaluate a situation for ourselves and (b) we have a certain freedom of choice - so being 'told' what to do takes our autonomy away from us.

Asking people what they could have done differently will mean that they learn for themselves, analysing the situation from the outside, and thinking through the results of doing something different. The brain learns so fast that all these extra choices will be coded and filed away for the next occasion - rather than their having to make a conscious effort to remember: 'next time this happens, I must........'

Another thing that we need to be aware of is that the unconscious mind does not process negatives.

DO NOT TURN THE PAGE until you have read this paragraph properly

DO THINK ABOUT THE NEXT PAGE while you are reading the next paragraph

What happens? Are you now insatiably curious about what is on the next page?

Had it crossed your mind to skip this paragraph before I put the idea into your head? DON'T WORRY! There's nothing difficult on the next page. How can you not worry? Because you have to think about being worried, in order not to do it.

- Don't look now........
- Don't laugh.......

are guaranteed to have the opposite effect to what you intended, and so the trick is to phrase things in the positive.

Negative	Positive
Don't forget	Remember
Don't tell anyone	This is confidential
Don't oversleep	Wake up in good time
Don't stay out too late	Come home at a reasonable time
Don't lose your cool	Keep your cool
Don't spill it	Be careful, it's very full

The language of broadcasting has changed: I was listening to some interviews from the BBC archives the other day, and the language patterns were beautiful. There was no knowing best, no 'holier than thou' attitude - whereas I find the current use of 'right/wrong', 'good/bad', 'should/ought to' seriously boring (and 'boring' is the most condemnatory thing I can say about anything).

I also have a theory that the media are creating serious divisions in our society: it would appear that, for them, everything must be either black or white - shades of grey seem to be beyond the pale. What sort of language patterns make you feel uncomfortable? Watch the television, listen to the radio, read the papers and listen to anyone talking, and you will soon become aware of what pushes your buttons. Ask your friends, and find out the patterns that offend most of them; it is interesting to discover how people use patterns that they admit to not liking when they are used on them.

(And, while you are becoming aware of language patterns that make you feel uncomfortable, you can also ask yourself what behaviours cause you discomfort when people are communicating with you, for example: what happens when someone points their finger at you? Or talks to you with their arms folded? Or with their hands on their hips? Or without looking at you? Or eyeball to eyeball? Or addresses you - as Queen Victoria said - like a public meeting? Ask your friends the same question and see what they come up with. Then you can adapt your behaviour accordingly.)

The interesting thing about language is that, if we change the way we use it, we change the way we think. I have a scheme that is going to make me very rich: every time my clients use 'should' or 'ought to' on somebody else, they owe me £5; and, every time they use either of them on themselves they owe me £50. Once we start being aware of the language we are using to give ourselves a hard time, like: 'I know I should go on a diet', 'I know it's wrong to think like that', 'I am bad at languages/maths - whatever', and so on - making ourselves feel more and more guilty by the minute - we begin to think of more respectful and productive ways in which we can address ourselves, and other people.

A final thought about communication. How do you think about it? What metaphor would you use for the possibly difficult discussion you are going to have with X? If you think of it as a battle, then a battle it will be; if you think of it as a game, it will be a game: if it is a Win/Win game, then that is great and, if it is Win/Lose, it could get nasty. If you think of it as a dance, what sort of dance will it be? A *Pas seul?* A *Pas de deux?* An eightsome reel? A country dance like Strip the Willow? What sort of dance do you know that you would like this dance to be?

Team Building

You could write this section yourself by combining what we have discussed so far, but I will save you some of the trouble by reminding you of some useful ways of thinking about teams.

Like everything else we have talked about, a team is a system which has a purpose and the first thing that we need to do is to discover the purpose. What is the team outcome? What will that give us? And what will we lose?

For example, one of the polo teams I worked with just wanted to win their matches, because it would make them feel good. That was fine, we went for it. The problems arose later: when they qualified to play at the championships at Cowdray (the highlight of their polo year), they discovered that - because they had won so many matches - they had been moved up a league; that the competition was now far greater than they were used to; and that matches were now not just there for the taking. It was only in hindsight that they realised that, although they had not done as well as they had expected at Cowdray, the experience of playing against better teams had done wonders for their game.

We can use a Christmas Tree to clarify our outcomes: to make sure that we really know what we want. As usual, start at the bottom, with 'What do we want?' and work up.

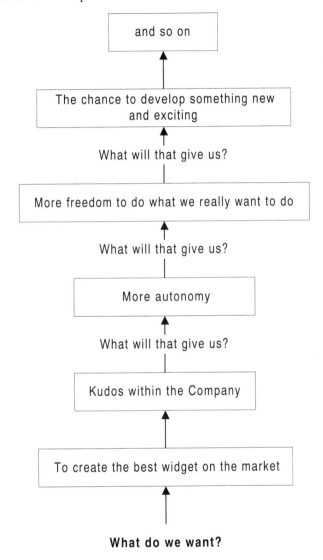

If we do this as a team, then everyone is involved, and thus a part of the dreams and the decisions.

The other thing that we need to think about is individual outcomes: what does each member of the team want for him or her self, within the team? One may want the chance to develop her own ideas; another may want to learn from the more experienced members and then move on; a third may just want to feel as though he belongs as part of the greater plan; a fourth may want to be involved with every part of the project; a fifth may want to specialise in one part of the project, and so on.

Everyone needs to do their own Christmas Tree, and each member of the team needs to know what every other member's outcomes are. In this way, not only will they know who to call on when they need help, they can also work together to further their own and each other's outcomes.

If we think back to Elton Mayo's experiment with working conditions and output, and to our presupposition that people make the best choices that they can according to the information that they have available to them, and to the section in 'Relationships' about how we know that someone values/ appreciates us, we will realise that each team member also needs to know every one else's evidence procedure for being a valued member of this team, for example:

- Does A need a cup of tea, when he is looking harassed?
- Does B need to go for a walk, when her brain seizes?
- Does C need a picture of a smiling face when he has done something well?
- Does D need a hug when she has made a mistake?
- Does E need to be left completely alone, when absorbed in a project?

We are all different, and the only way we will find out what people need from us is by asking.

Think back to the time when you belonged to a team that achieved its outcome with maximum effect and minimum fuss: what was going on inside you at that time? How did you know what was needed? How did you make that connection with everyone else in the team? Ask the other members of the team the same questions, and you will discover your own strategies for making teams work.

And, while we are on the subject of teams: the most important team of all is your own - all those different parts of you that want nothing but the best for you. Consult your team first because, if they are working together before you start, then everything else falls into place.

Creativity

Let's go back to our widget that is better than any other widget on the market. What will the effect of this outcome be? Will we become the only successful widget makers in the market? Will people be able to afford our widgets? Will we have to increase and expand our production lines? What will we lose? Will our company have to devote itself entirely to widget production? What will then happen if someone else then produces a better widget? And so on.

Having thought through the effects, we can then use Walt Disney's strategy to think about our outcome. Robert Dilts used to work with Disney, and he modelled his strategy for turning dreams into reality. They used to say that there were three Disneys: the Dreamer, the Realist and the Critic, and the only problem with this was that you never knew which one was going to come to your meeting. The great thing about this strategy, as with all the stuff that Robert has developed, is that it separates our thinking into the right compartments.

You can use this strategy for team building within yourself: to get your own Dreamer, Realist and Critic working together. Each of these three has a valuable job to do and, unless we separate them, our internal critic may pop up and put the dampers upon any brilliant idea almost before we recognise that it is a brilliant idea - by telling us that we are not capable of achieving it - or something equally unhelpful. All that we need to remember is that it is our internal critic's job to keep us out of trouble, and that it is doing this in the best way it knows. The Disney strategy gives our Critic as much time and space as our Dreamer and our Realist; and, once our Critic knows that we are giving it the proper amount of respect and attention, then it can take its time and contribute in a valuable way, rather than acting out of panic in order to keep us safe.

With a team, you need a fairly large room with an area for dreaming, an area for realism and an area for criticism. It is also very useful to have people to put all the ideas onto flip charts. You can do your dreaming sitting down, or you can do it standing up and moving about. (A lot of people moving about and dreaming out loud produces something fairly close to Bedlam, but movement of the body creates even more free-flowing thought.)

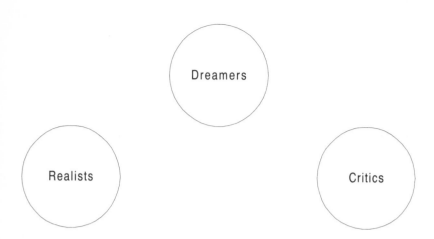

Dreaming mode is visual: people will be looking up at their internal pictures; their breathing will be fairly high in their chests, and they will probably talk fairly fast, as they try to keep up with the ideas that come pouring in.

The important thing to remember here is that dreaming is inviolable: dreaming is all that people are allowed to do in this part of the room, and at this time; that the dreams can be as wild and crazy as anybody wants; and that everything in the room was once the result of somebody's dream: once there were no chairs, no tables, no carpets, no buildings - they were all figments of somebody's imagination. Nothing in the room existed before somebody dreamed it up.

When the dreaming is done, it is time for everyone to move to the Realists' part of the room. The Realists are going to look at the dream, in its space, and ask and answer the 'how' questions: *how are we going to achieve this?* The Realists are the logistics experts: they arrange for the right people to do the right things in the right places at the right time. They are going to look at the dream, from a detached position, and decide *how* the dream is going to be fulfilled. They may well stand like the film directors in our earlier experiments: leaning back slightly, with one arm across the body and the other hand supporting the chin, as they discuss matters with themselves and other people. Maybe some parts of the dream are physically impossible to fulfil: the Realists can make modifications.

When the Realists have finished, everyone moves into the Critic's position, and there are two important things to remember here:

The Critics' job is to criticise the Dream: the Dreamers have been given the task of being as wild and wacky as they want. We have now separated the Dream from the Dreamers, and it is *only the Dream* that comes under scrutiny.

The Critics are there to find out what will not work, and why. Theirs is an important, *constructive* job.

As they look at the Dream, the Critics may have their arms folded, and may have their heads on one side as they discuss the pros and cons of the dream with themselves. Again, modifications may need to be made to the dream.

Once the Critics have finished, everyone moves back into the modified Dream, and experiences the adjustments that have been suggested, in order to make it work even better.

Then they move into the Realists' spot again, and amend their plans, according to the adjustments which have been made to the Dream.

From there, they move to Critics again, to see what the Dream looks like now that the adjustments have been made.

The team can move around from spot to spot until the Dreamers, the Realists and the Critics are all content: when everyone realises that everything will work, and work well.

Once this is done, it is a good plan to walk the triangle (maybe turning it into a circle), several times, so that all three components: dreaming, realism and criticism become integrated - both symbolically and physically.

One of the many advantages of doing things this way is that the whole team is involved in the creation of the dream: everyone has contributed and everyone knows what is happening and why. And you can, of course, do it on your own to turn your individual dreams into reality.

Motivation

Because we presuppose that people make the best choices that they can according to the information that they have available to them at the time, the question of lack of motivation does not arise in our team: everyone knows exactly what is going on; everyone knows that they are a vital component of their team; everyone knows that they belong, that they matter.

Dealing with Difficult People

Outside our team, things may be different; we may need contact with people who have entirely different models of the world from ours. In the course of getting our project up and running, we may come up against X who seems to be deliberately obstructive.

We have our presupposition that X's behaviour has a positive intention and our belief that X matters to us - not only from the project point of view, but also, and more importantly, as a person. These two will stand us in very good stead and, if they are not quite enough, then we can use the Meta Mirror on 19, experiencing the situation with X from the different perceptual positions; and this will provide us with all the answers that we need.

Problem Solving

A problem only exists when the present state is different from the desired state. For example:

> **Desired State:**
> *profits up by 10%*

> **Present state:**
> *profits down by 10%*

You can use the SCORE model on page 84 to solve any sort of problem. The symptom is the present state, the outcome is the desired state.

Another model you can use is Robert and Todd's Jungle Gym.

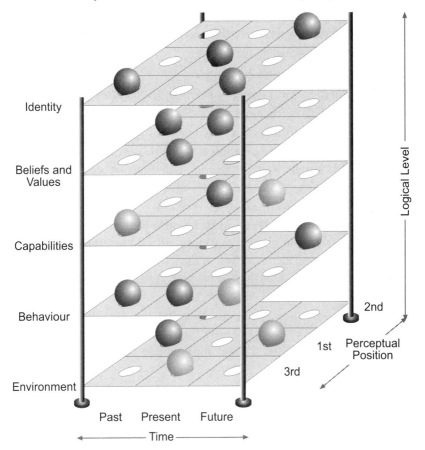

Jungle Gym

As you can see, this is the three dimensional version of all the things that we have been talking about: logical levels, perceptual positions and time.

Of course, the ideal would be to have a structure that you can climb about inside - a colleague has one in her garden, so that she can literally move herself from one position to another - but I chose to have a little one made (measuring 12" x 12" x 18"), and each of the 45 squares has a hole in it which can hold a ping-pong ball. I have some ordinary, white ping-pong balls and also lots of brightly coloured balls which are the same size.

So let's put our problem into the Jungle Gym:

- The problem is Present: profits are down, now;
- It is at Capability level: we have not been able to maintain profits
- It is 1st Position: inside the company

Place a white ball in the appropriate hole

- The desired state is Future, 1st Position, Capabilities

Place a coloured ball in the appropriate hole

We now have 43 different positions from which we can choose to examine and experience our problem. What do we discover if we put a coloured ball into Past, Behaviour, 3rd Position and watch, as detached observers, what was going on in the past (before profits began to fall), and how people were behaving?

We can choose to go anywhere in the box that we like: we can go into 2nd Position with our main competitors, or our most important customers, at Belief or Identity level, in the past (before profits began to fall), and experience what they believe about the market, or about us; or how they think about themselves.

What will we discover about ourselves, if we go into the past in 1st Position, at Belief or Identity level? What did we believe about ourselves, about the Company, about our products, before profits started to fall?

If we go 2nd Position with some of our staff at the Capability level, what happens?

The more positions we use, the more we explore the problem, the more we will learn about it and the clearer the solution will become.

*****

If you want to move around within the problem, you can make a two-dimensional space by doing this on a staircase - preferably a nice, wide one: each step takes you up or down a logical level; the width of the staircase will give you the time span; or you can create enough space for 1st and 2nd position on the steps, and you can move to the edge of the staircase to get yourself outside the problem and into 3rd position.

Negotiation

We are involved in negotiation throughout our lives: from multi-million dollar deals, to who is going to put the cat out; and, after all we have discussed, you really don't need any input from me in this section. However, just in case you feel that your automatic hunch to go for outcomes (like we have done with everything else) must be too easy to be right, the double Christmas Tree on page 78, which we used to negotiate between different parts of ourselves, is exactly what you need to negotiate for Win/Win between apparently immovable factions.

The important thing to remember is that nobody is going to come to blows about behaviours - *although that may be what they are complaining about*: people come to blows about their beliefs and their identities - we only have to look at all the wars that have been fought in the name of religion to realise what happens when we threaten people's belief systems. When I first started my research for *Lazy Learning*, and was wildly excited about the things I was discovering, some people in the teaching profession could not get rid of me fast enough: here I was saying that learning was easy, whereas they had spent the whole of their lives being programmed that it was difficult: 'learning is difficult' was one of the beliefs upon which their identities as teachers was based.

Rather than the behaviours themselves, it is the *effect* of the behaviours that we need to think about, and the intention behind the behaviours. For example: why does X react so badly when Y turns up late for an appointment? Maybe it is because, for X, turning up late is evidence that she is not important enough to make an effort for. Who knows? And maybe Y thinks that, now that he and X know each other so well, the time has come to acknowledge this friendship by relaxing normal strict codes about punctuality. This is why we need to separate the behaviour from the intention and, where possible, discover what the intention is

And remember that we also need to separate the people from the problem: sitting opposing factions down, face to face and eyeball to eyeball can immediately create a chance for confrontation if internal states are bad, and each side is feeling hard done by before you start. (Some people may insist upon sitting face to face because they think that they can gather more information if they can 'see' as much as possible of the other person; they have forgotten that (a) they have four more senses apart from their eyes and (b) their peripheral vision - what they see out of the corners of their eyes - can pick up all sorts of information that focussed vision may miss.)

We say that someone is 'on our side' for a reason; and, if we can get the protagonists working side by side - maybe sitting down, or even walking along while they talk - we have created the situation where they are - physically at least - 'on the same side'. And, supposing they are sitting down, we can write the problem up on a flip chart, which will distance them from it even more effectively.

Getting people moving is a great help - this is why walking and talking is an effective way to solve a problem: if the body is moving, the brain is moving and thinking can flow; if the body is stuck in one place, the brain is stuck too. Someone with their arms folded, saying: 'my position is........' means exactly that: they have no intention of changing their position - physically or mentally.

Above all: it is Win/Win that we are going for - the very best, and more, for all parties. Here is an imaginary scenario: A makes components and B makes machines. They are haggling over a price. As usual, start at the bottom.

Now that the cards are on the table, we discover that both A and B want to develop their ideas, and that A wants to develop a better, cheaper widget - which can only be good for B. At this level they can co-operate, if they want to: maybe they can share findings from their research; maybe their R & D teams can work together; who knows what ideas they will come up with - to the advantage of both parties for the future? Or maybe they will want to go even further up the levels, to discover more about each other's dreams and plans.

And, if they had never bothered to ask the questions, they would never have discovered what benefits each could provide for the other. As we all know, the whole is infinitely greater than the sum of its parts.

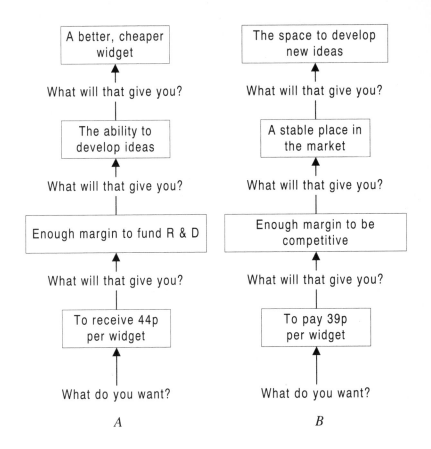

A

B

Leadership

What do you want from a leader? What sort of person would you follow? What qualities do you expect from someone who is going to take you into the future? Stop and think about it for a bit: who are the people who have been the leaders in your life? What was so special about each one? How did they treat you? How did they treat other people? And what did they all have in common? Make yourself a list, and then ask family, friends and colleagues the same questions, so that you can find the overall pattern.

What is the difference that makes the difference between someone whose dream people will commit themselves to, and someone whom you would not follow anywhere?

These are mostly behaviour-level questions; and I am sure that, in the course of your research, you will discover that there is something about these leaders that you may not be able to define so precisely: something inside you that knows that they believe in and are committed to their dream - which makes you believe that the dream is worth pursuing.

To find out how they do this, remember all the times when you have been an effective leader: those occasions when you have been so engaged, aligned and committed to whatever it was that you wanted to do, that everything and everybody has just seemed to fall into place around you. We are not talking about a grand crusade: it could be a party you decided to give or organise; a family outing; a collection for charity; a meeting of friends - any and all of those occasions when you have taken the initiative and carried it through.

Once you have got a good selection, you can write down all the logical levels on different pieces of paper:

Mission Identity Beliefs Capabilities Behaviour Environment

and lay them out in a line along the floor. You are going to rediscover what was going on inside you at each level of these occasions when you were a leader. Select the occasion you are most proud of, and step into Environment, taking that occasion with you.

Ask yourself the questions: 'Where am I?' and 'When is this happening?' You are back there, in that time: seeing what you see; hearing what you hear; feeling what you feel; tasting what you taste and smelling what you smell.

Describe it all - out loud, pretending that I am there with you - at that time, so that I too can experience and enjoy what you are experiencing and enjoying at every level.

Then you can move into Behaviour, and describe exactly what you are doing to fulfil this dream of yours, and what way others are reacting to what you are doing. For example, you might be dreaming about it, then talking to other people about it and then taking action.

The next step is into Capabilities: *how* are you, say, creating this dream, inspiring other people, and so on? What are you seeing, hearing, feeling, tasting and smelling in order to be able to do all this?

And, when you are aware, through every system, of just *how* you are doing what you are doing, you can step into Beliefs, and ask yourself why you are doing all this. What deeply-held beliefs are creating this dream and carrying it through into reality?

And now you can step into Identity. *Who* are you in this system that you have created? This system where things are happening according to your ideas? It may be easier to use a metaphor - to describe yourself figuratively, rather than literally: you might be a flaming torch, a catalyst, a resource centre, a gardener - only you will have the right answer for who you are.

And, when you are completely aware of who you are in this system, you can step into Mission, taking that awareness with you, and ask yourself what this dream of yours is achieving, and will achieve, for other people: it might be for your nearest and dearest; it might be for friends or colleagues; it might be for the planet - I don't know: it's your mission; and, as you stand in the Mission space, you can experience that engagement, that alignment and that commitment in every cell of your body and *know* what it is to be a leader.

If you want to, you can do this with all the other occasions from the list you made earlier. There are two good reasons for doing this:

1. You will become even more aware of how effective you are as a leader
2. You will discover what happens in common in each position, on each occasion.

So now you have the structure of your own leadership, and you can play around with this in all sorts of ways.

For example, you could write another set of logical levels and place them parallel to the one you have just used: these are going to be your next project.

Then, working your way up the set you have done, and re-experiencing what went on at every level, you could instruct the 'you' on the parallel set about what will be going on at each level in your new project: what that 'you' will be seeing, hearing, feeling, tasting and smelling at each level - as you and your team turn your latest idea into reality.

And when you have got to Mission on the original set, you can then

step across into your new Mission, taking all your engagement, align-
ment and commitment with you - into your new project; and, from
there, work your way down - slowly and carefully - through Identity,
Beliefs, Capabilities, Behaviours and Environment, until you have got
the whole process into your neurology at every level.

Or, you can just start in Environment, with your new project, work
your way up to Mission level, and then take all the goodies that you
have gathered on the way up all the way down again - through each
level, until you are back in Environment fully equipped, with every
resource you could possibly need, to lead your team into action.

You can also play around with any of the techniques that you have already
learned, and see what you discover. For example, some years ago, Marcelo
and I were playing around with the SCORE Model; Marcelo was thinking
about Rosie (whom I had not yet met) and I was - less romantically - thinking about my belief that I could not get support for my ideas about learning
because I was too insignificant. Robert and Todd had suggested that we
write:

Symptom   Cause   Outcome   Resources   Effects

on different pieces of paper and lay them out on the floor, in any order or
position that we chose, and try moving them (and ourselves) around, and
changing the order to see what else we came up with by way of ideas.
Marcelo was making suggestions about where I put my bits of paper, just to
see what would happen, and I discovered - to my delight - that my so-called
'Cause' - insignificance - was, in fact, a Resource: in other words, I was so
insignificant that the education system would not notice my presence until
after the *Lazy Learning* message had got through, which was my outcome.
(And, for the romantically inclined: the next time we met, Marcelo proudly
introduced me to his beautiful bride, Rosie.)

Irresistible Presentations

We need to ask ourselves the same sort of questions about Presentation as
we asked about Leadership: what is it about a presenter and a presentation
that works for us? When I ask people on presentation courses these questions, they often come up with the answers that they think they 'ought to
come up with', like:

- The Presenter knows his/her facts

- Lots of information

in other words, all sorts of objective stuff. Their own presentations have reflected these beliefs and are frequently utterly forgettable.

So let's stop, and think subjectively for a moment. Think about the presenters who have really impressed you. What is it about them, and what is it about the way they put their stuff over, that grabs and holds your attention? You might like to make a list, and to consult friends and colleagues, so that you can find the overall structure that grabs and holds everybody's attention.

An audience is made up of human beings, and - as we know - human beings react subjectively first and objectively later (which is sometimes too late). Some questions to start you off:

- Did they involve you in their presentation?
- Did they make you laugh?
- Did they make you think you were important?
- Did they relate complicated stuff to something simple that everyone could understand?
- Were they interested in what they were talking about?
- Did they believe what they were saying?
- Were they people you would like to get to know better?

And, if 'yes' to these last two, how did you know?

(A colleague was telling me how disappointed he'd been by a presentation given by another colleague: 'He was concentrating on a woman in the front row, and I kept wanting to say: "Hey! I'm here too!" - I know I shouldn't feel like that...'. I could relate to what he was saying, because I'd been at the same presentation. And, of course, he had every right to feel that way: we experience what we experience - whether we 'should' or 'shouldn't'. I did not ask the presenter what the positive intention of that particular communication was; all I know is that the response that he got was not favourable.)

And while all that bubbles in your unconscious mind, you can think consciously about your beliefs about audiences; for example: when you walk into a room full of people, you can choose to believe that they will tear you limb from limb (which is physically possible), or you can choose to believe that you are all going to have a lot of fun.

What would be the most useful belief to have before and during a presentation?

You can also ask yourself some questions as though you were a member of the audience; for example:

- Have you come specially to give the speaker a hard time?
- Are you determined to find fault with everything the speaker says or does?
- Are you completely uninterested in the subject anyway?
- Are you going to stand up and say that the speaker is an idiot?
- Are you going to cause a riot?

Or

- Are you there because:
- > the speaker has something that you want?
- > you are interested in the subject?
- > you are expecting to enjoy yourself?

Why do *you* go to a presentation? As before: ask your friends and colleagues the same questions, to find the overall pattern of expectations.

And then you can do a little more second position thinking about your audience.

- What do you like to experience, as an individual who is part of a group of people?
- Do you often feel like a complete idiot, compared to everybody else who is there?
- Do you feel that any question you might want to ask could be considered as stupid/unnecessary/unimportant?
- What does the presenter need to do to make you feel good about yourself?

Once you have the structure of a good presentation, and presupposing that you know enough about your subject to be able to put it across, all you need to remember is:

1. People process information in different ways, so they would like to hear what you have to say, see what you mean and experience it for themselves. In other words, give it to them in all systems. You can conjure up pictures, sounds, feelings, tastes and smells

with words; you can give them visual aids; you can give them things to play with or pass things round for them to feel, as well as look at. People like to be involved at every level, so that they can truly appreciate the value of what you are offering them.

2. People can only process a certain amount of information: if there is too much, their brains will go into overload and lose the lot. I know that your subject is utterly fascinating, and that you are longing to share everything with everybody: resist the temptation! For example, for a 15-minute presentation, give them a maximum of four (preferably three) good bites at your apple - just enough to whet their appetites, and make them long to know more. You can have handouts and questions at the end to fill in any gaps for them.

3. These people matter to you as people, rather than as statisticians, geographers, linguists, graphic designers - or whatever group they represent as your audience.

4. Anyone who asks a difficult question, or even disagrees with you, has a positive intention: if you can't answer a question, you can always say: 'I don't know' and, if they disagree with you, that is because you have different maps of the world - and it's fun to do some map swapping.

5. You are applying the principles of Neuro-*Linguistic* Programming to your presentation; when you *present* something to someone, you are giving them a *present*.

Armed with all this (which you have always known anyway, deep down inside you), you can use the logical levels again, in the same way that you used them for Leadership. Because I like to do things the easy way (for me, once the 'who else?' is clearly defined, then the rest falls into place), I prefer to start at the top - in the Mission space - with the questions:

'What changes to people's thinking do I want to create with
this presentation?
And what will that give them?'

Maybe I want to create more choices in the way that they think about things; maybe I want to create the experience of feeling okay about themselves;

maybe I want them to discover that they feel good when they are kind to themselves.

What it will give *them* is the chance to make their lives simpler, and more fun - if that is what they would like (and I need to remember that - for some people - a simple, fun life might be the last thing they want).

As you did with Leadership, you can answer all your questions out loud - either for yourself, or pretending that you are telling me all about this presentation.

When you have got your outcome for the audience aligned in your body, so that all of you is completely committed to it, you can step into

Identity and ask yourself:

Who am I, in this role, with this mission, for these people?

As before, you might find it easier to use a metaphor in this space. Maybe you are a basket of goodies that they can pick and choose from; maybe you are a toyshop with new ideas for them to play with; maybe you are a guiding light - only you will know the answer to this question.

Once you have found an identity that you are completely comfortable with as the presenter of this fascinating topic, you can move into the Beliefs space, and ask yourself questions like:

- Why am I presenting this particular stuff to these people?
- Why will it be useful for them?
- Why are they here?

When you have the answers to these questions, and to any other 'why' questions that you want to ask, you can move into Capabilities and ask yourself things like:

- How am I getting into rapport with these people?
- How am I grabbing their interest?
- How am I presenting this? Low key? Lots of hype? Enthusiastically?
- How am I responding to questions?
- How am I getting this particular point across?

and all the other 'how' questions you will need to ask about your presentation. What is going on inside you to enable you to do all these things?

This is an interesting spot: spend time in it and you will discover all sorts of fascinating questions and answers about how you do things.

For example, you will discover that, when you are in rapport with people, your eyes are relaxed so that you can take everything in your peripheral vision, picking up all the smiles and nods, and all the unconscious signals that people give when they are enjoying themselves; you will discover that there really is no separation between you and them: they want something that you are giving them, and so the connection is firmly established; you will discover that ideas and information seem to come to you out of nowhere in response to questions - I won't spoil it for you by revealing any more.

After you have spent as long as you need in this space, you can move into Behaviours, and ask yourself questions like:

- What am I wearing?
- What am I doing?
- Am I standing or sitting?
- Am I speaking loudly or softly; fast or slowly?
- Am I enjoying myself?
- Am I looking at my audience?
- Am I talking to them? Or am I 'telling' them?
- Am I giving them time to process what I am saying?
- What is going on inside me?
- What am I seeing, hearing, feeling, tasting and smelling?

and every other question you can think of about what you are doing in order to get your message across in the effective and enjoyable way that you would like.

And finally, step into Environment, and ask:

- Where am I making this presentation?
- When is this happening?
     Look around:
- How big is the room?
- Where are you in relation to your audience?
- How many people are there?
- Are they comfortable?

- Where is the light coming from?

What else do you notice?

Of course, if you prefer, you can start at Environment and work your way up to Mission, and then down again, to bring everything that goes with your mission back to the Environment space. You will know what is best for you.

Another interesting thing to do is to walk along parallel to your logical levels' line and observe yourself from the outside, in each position. Detached from your performance, you will be able to see if there is anything else you need to do to make it even better.

One last thing: remember your magic button? This is an ideal moment to use it: press it just before you step out in front of your audience, or at whatever the right moment is for you - and enjoy your self!

Health and Happiness

I do a lot of work with health - both with animals and humans. With animals, it is just straight 'hands on' stuff; but humans, for some extraordinary reason, do not necessarily believe that all they need to do is simply allow themselves to heal themselves. This is where the presuppositions of NLP come particularly useful, because they add to our choices.

If we know, at the deepest level, that every behaviour, however bizarre, has a positive intention, then we can consider any illness simply as a communication from the unconscious to the conscious mind that all is not well.

This section is just to stretch your mind a bit, to discover how NLP can be applied effectively in any situation. I have also selected some case histories which, to me, show a wonderful variety of positive intentions (some of them were so beautiful that they almost reduced me to tears), in order to demonstrate the lengths that the unconscious mind will go to in order to look after its owner.

The body is an endlessly adaptable system; for example, astronauts spend a long time in a weightless condition: they move through space using their hands - rather like swimming - and, as a result, their spines allow themselves to stretch. One woman's spine was 2" longer when she came back to earth.

James

James asked me to work with his asthma, which only came on at night, and only when he was at home, in his own bed. We went back to the time it had started - in his twenties: at that time, he was under a lot of pressure. 'Aha!', I thought to myself 'he couldn't cope with the strain.' So I asked how he had felt about that pressure, and had a rapid reminder of the dangers of snap judgements: he had loved every minute of it!

Back on course, I asked what else had been going on in his life at that time, and it transpired that that was when his wife had been told that she could never have a child. She was shattered, and James was probably even more shattered for her than he was for himself; and, when I asked him to ask the asthma what its positive intention was, the answer came: 'To give my wife someone to care for'. It had done a wonderful job - James really appreciated it; and they agreed that it could now be retired.

Angela

Angela was another client with asthma, so I asked her if she wanted to do anything about it. She looked at me in horror and said: 'Oh! No! If I didn't have asthma, I'd have to do sport at school!' I asked if the asthma came on at sports time every day. She said 'No'; but she'd fake it, if it didn't. I suggested having fake asthma instead of real the thing anyway, as it would be much easier and much better for her. And this was all that she needed to give her more choices in how to react.

An interesting thought: people often talk about 'having an asthma attack'. Phrased like this, it presupposes that the asthma is in charge; that it is the asthma which decides when it is, or is not, going to attack. If we follow this to its logical conclusion, the person with asthma becomes a 'victim' of an outside force. On the same subject: if someone says 'I am asthmatic', this is an identity-level statement - presupposing: 'this is me - this is who I am: so there's nothing to be done'.

If we have to talk about what comes under the label of 'asthma', it is much more helpful to discuss what actually happens, for example: the person has difficulty breathing - this is a capability, and we can do something about our capabilities.

Sarah

Sarah had rheumatoid arthritis, or some such crippling disease - I am not good at labels because I'm interested in the person, rather than the name of the disease. As often happens, people come to me as a last resort and, by the time I saw Sarah, she was in a pretty bad way. It had all started with an attack of 'flu, and then suddenly she found herself crippled. As usual, I asked what had been going on in her life before the disease appeared, and she said that she'd asked herself this question over and over again, and had come up with nothing. Her marriage was happy, her job was interesting and she and her husband were looking forward to a climbing holiday.

Curious, I asked her whether she enjoyed climbing and discovered that she loved it: she regaled me with tales of the things that she had climbed as a child, which would have given her mother apoplexy if she had known. And then she suddenly said - covering her eyes with her bandaged hands: 'Oh, my God! I'd forgotten!' And what she had forgotten was that, on their last climbing holiday, her husband had frozen on a ledge 300 feet up and, for four hours, she had thought that she was going to lose him. After it was all over, she said to herself: 'I never want to go through that again'.

So when she blithely booked another climbing holiday, her unconscious said: 'Oi! You said you never wanted to go through that again', and gave her 'flu. But she paid no attention to the message and so, in desperation, it did the only thing it could think of to make absolutely sure that she never went climbing with her husband again: it crippled her.

As we talked, and as she paid attention to what her unconscious wanted her to learn, she began to move more freely: the disease had done its job, and she could allow herself to let it go.

Believing in Our Health

Your body is a self-healing system: if it weren't, you would have died of 'flu - or bled to death from a cut - years ago.

Try an experiment:

Think about something which you know will heal itself - whether you take any medicine, or not: something like a cut finger, or a cold, or a broken bone.

Then think about a disease that is 'supposed' to kill us: like cancer, or aids.

Then compare those two sets of pictures, in your mind's eye:

- Where do you see the self-healing ones?
- Where do you see the supposed killers?
- What size is each picture?
- How close to you is each picture?
- What differences are there in colour, size, shape, focus, etc?

You will find that you have two different files, and that you represent these two concepts in completely different ways. And the interesting thing is that, when you move a supposed killer into the 'self-healing' file - making the pictures exactly the same size, quality, distance away from you, and so on, interesting things happen - like you heal yourself.

My bible, when I am working with health, is Deepak Chopra's *Quantum Healing* (see the Bibliography). Chopra is a 'proper' Doctor, that is to say he trained in the States and became Chief of Staff at the New England

Memorial Hospital in Stoneham, Massachusetts. He then had the good for-
tune to spend time with the Maharishi Mahesh Yogi - the founder of Tran-
scendental Meditation - who gave him a series of mental techniques from
Ayurveda, the ancient tradition of Indian medicine, and asked him to take
them back to the West and explain clearly and scientifically how they
worked.

So, when I am working with people who have had the belief firmly
installed that their disease is incurable, I can quote chunks of Chopra about,
say, how long it takes for the liver to renew itself (just six weeks); one cannot argue with a 'proper' doctor on matters of health, and so their beliefs
begin to shift before we start. And anyway, 'incurable' only means that the
doctors don't know how to cure it, yet.

Robert Dilts has a theory that lawsuits against medical practitioners have
become such a nightmare in the States that insurance companies insist that
patients be given the entire list of every complication, and everything that
might possibly go wrong; and so, instead of being able to concentrate on
healing their patients, doctors are obliged to give them what Stephen Gilligan would call a 'diagnostic induction' to develop complications - which
would otherwise never have crossed their minds; for example, you cut your
finger and there is a possibility you might get gangrene.

Give me animals to work with any day! They don't ask stupid questions,
and nobody has told them that what we are going to do cannot possibly
work. They just put themselves into trance, help themselves to the energy
that is coming out of my hands, and heal themselves. And, when they are
done, they simply come out of trance and wander off.

In *The Psychobiology of Mind-Body Healing*, Rossi talks about 'the like-
able Mr Wright' who was considered terminally ill with lymphosarcoma,
and had developed a resistance to all known palliative treatments. He was
febrile, gasping for air and completely bedridden. His physician, Dr Philip
West, said that to give him a prognosis of more than two weeks seemed to
be stretching things.

A new 'wonder drug' was to be tested at the hospital, and Mr Wright
begged to be included in the trials; he did not qualify - not having a life
expectancy of six months or more. However, he was so determined that this
new drug would be the answer to everything that Dr West broke all the
rules, and allowed him to start the treatment of three injections a week. He

was given his first injection on a Friday and Dr West went home for the weekend, expecting him to be dead, or at least moribund by Monday.

Not a bit of it! By Monday, Mr Wright was up and about, and chatting to everybody; the tumour masses were half their original size and, within ten days, he was discharged from his death bed. None of the other patients on the trial had shown any improvement.

Then some reports came out, casting doubts on the efficacy of this 'wonder drug', and Mr Wright, who by now had enjoyed two months of almost perfect health, lost faith in his last hope and relapsed into his original state. Dr West, fascinated, decided that it could not harm the dying Mr Wright in any way if he were to play the quack; and so he told him that the drug he had been given had deteriorated on standing, and that a new batch was being delivered the next day. Mr Wright immediately returned to optimism and Dr West invented a two-day delay for the fictitious shipment, in order to increase his excitement. Then, with great ceremony, he injected this '*fresh, doubly potent*' preparation - which consisted of *fresh water*, and nothing more.

This time the results were even more dramatic than before: Mr Wright recovered even faster and - the picture of health - remained symptom free for over two months.

And then, the AMA announced that the drug which he believed had cured him had proved to be 'worthless' in treatment of cancer. Within a few days, Mr Wright was admitted to hospital in *extremis* and, two days later, he was dead.

What will You Lose when You Get Better?

I asked this question of a client who used to have aids. The answer was, 'People doing my shopping for me'; I hate shopping with a passion, so I could relate to this. Shortly afterwards, Edward - one of the faithful band of shoppers - called in. 'Edward', I said, 'will you still do Peter's shopping when he hasn't got aids any more?' 'No way!' came the answer. So Peter had to think a little more deeply, and come up with all the important things that he had discovered by being so seriously ill: like the fact that his father loved him (which he had not known).

A colleague used to have 'flu every three months or so, until he stopped to consult himself about the positive intention. And the positive intention was: you work much too hard - you need two days in bed, every three months or so. And so now he books his 'flu: he asks his staff if it will be okay if he has 'flu on, say, Wednesday and Thursday next week. If this would mess them about, they find another two days. The result is that he has his two days in bed, every three months, and comes back to work fresh as a daisy - instead of feeling as though he has been run over by a steamroller, as the aftermath of 'flu; and he has never had 'flu since.

A friend, who has had a series of strokes, was telling me how she has gradually discovered all the things that don't matter. For example, first she discovered it did not matter a jot that the table napkins were not starched (a shocking state of affairs, that she would never have contemplated before she was ill); and then she discovered that there are actually some very high quality paper napkins on the market. She is enjoying being a true 'Warrior' - living each day as if it were her last - and consequently discovering more and more of the wonderful things that the world and all its inhabitants have to offer.

I asked a client, who had continually failed her driving test through 'nerves', what she would lose if she had a driving licence. The answer was the weekly shopping trips with her husband: he was a very hard-working, self-employed man and the only time that he was guaranteed to spend with her was Saturday mornings. She justifiably felt that, once she no longer needed to be driven to the shops, she would lose this precious time with him. The matter was negotiated: she passed her test the next time, and they now spend their Saturday mornings doing much nicer things than shopping.

By-passing the Conscious Mind

While it is not our business to interfere with anybody who really wants to hang onto their illness, or to die, some people are quite determined, at the conscious level, that nothing can be done about their disease - because they believe what other people have told them; so we sometimes need to be a little bit sneaky, if we truly believe that they want to heal themselves.

Anthony was very overweight, and had a bad back (as the result of an old rugby injury) which was driving him and his family mad, because it would 'go out' the moment there was anything important to do: his wife was having to win all the bread, and she had had enough of having to support the whole family, on her own. He asked me casually one day if I wanted to 'have a go at' him, adding that he had no faith in me anyway. So I suggested he settle himself somewhere comfortable and not to try to *pay attention* to what I was saying, and so he slid into a nice easy trance, while I told him a modified version of the story about the Persian Rug, which you will come to later; I also put in something about how he would become the weight that he wanted to be - naturally and easily. When I'd finished, he told me proudly that he'd done what I'd told him, and paid no attention to what I was saying, then he left: consciously determined that he *was* not *going to change*.

But his unconscious mind knew better, and took charge. When I saw him, by chance, six months later, there was this bouncing, vibrant, lean, healthy-looking man. 'You look good!', I said. 'Oh, yes', he said, off-handedly, 'nothing to do with you, of course. I just stopped wanting to eat fattening food, and my back just stopped hurting'. I love it when a plan comes together! And I certainly wasn't going to spoil things by explaining what I had done. Also, he was quite right: it was nothing to do with me - his body had simply taken charge, and healed itself.

Story-telling is a very good way of by-passing the conscious mind: a story is just a story, - nobody is 'telling' you what to do - you can take it or leave it. And, if you choose to take it, you can adapt it to suit yourself - because it is only a story. The other thing about stories is that the conscious mind may well think that it is beneath its dignity to listen to anything that is not strictly factual, so it will think about something 'more important' - leaving the unconscious free to take in the message and profit from it.

Weight Problems

Weight problems are fascinating if we look for positive intentions. For some people, eating is the way they make themselves feel good: food is a present from them to themselves. It gives them the occasion to acknowledge who they are. For others, weight may give 'weight' to who they are: or make them 'solid' citizens; or give them a larger safe space to inhabit.

There is the story about the woman who felt that, if she lost weight and became streamlined and elegant, other men would fancy her and this would put her marriage in jeopardy.

A friend of mine is on a diet which I would consider to be the next best thing to starvation, and she is still overweight (according to the rules). When she used to be seriously round and cuddly, her husband would tell her that she was worth at least 8 cows to him - so she does not want to devalue herself too much in his eyes.

And when we think about the way that we talk about 'losing' weight, as though weight were something important for us to have, it is not surprising that part of us feels that we do not want to let it go. And it is interesting to remember that the Brits calculate their weight in pounds - the same words as ££££ - and who wants to 'lose £££££'?

If we know that people have, within them, all the resources that they need, we can work with the positive intention and arrange for Win/Win. In other words, if the positive intention is to feel safe and self-confident, then we can create the state where the person knows, at the deepest level, that they are who they are, and they are okay; and, once this has happened, they can allow the excessive weight to melt away - naturally and easily.

The important thing about weight is to discover, at the beginning, what weight would be best for us - by going back to a time when we felt really good and fit and healthy, at a certain weight. Because the unconscious mind will do *exactly* as it is asked, we need to be completely precise: a client of mine simply instructed herself to lose weight - it was something that *she* could do for *her self*; and so lose it she did - ending up a bag of bones, with black hands and feet, in a mental hospital: her body had its instructions (and the 'why': a present from *her* to *her self*), and it was going to obey them *at any price*. Had she given instructions as to the exact weight she wanted to be, things would have been different.

Hereditary Diseases?

I was lunching with friends, one day, and there was a young man there whose whole appearance from the back threatened stress, building up to a heart attack. After lunch, we were chatting about this and that, and he told me that the one fear in his life was that, because he was so like his father, he would have a heart attack (his father, whom he adored, had died of one).

When we are young, we model ourselves on other people in order to learn how to behave, and how to fit into the system. Watch little girls behaving exactly like their mothers; and little boys exactly like their fathers. Have you ever noticed how like a parent an adopted child can be? I remember being given a terrible rocket by my mother - at the age of about five - for answering the telephone by saying: 'Clifford speaking' (Clifford was my maiden name): this was no way for a young lady to behave. 'Clifford speaking' was how my father answered the telephone - I modelled my father (he taught me to do all those fun things that boys do), and therefore it never occurred to me that everything he did might not be 'right'.

There was a wonderful story in 1995 about two little boys, aged two and three, who decided to take the family cat for a drive in their father's car. Simply by modelling their father, they by-passed three anti-theft devices, started the car and set off down the road. There was a photograph of them in the paper, bouncing up and down, and having a wonderful time at the wheel, enjoying themselves to pieces - being grown-up.

We can take on other people's stuff, lock, stock and barrel. In NLP we work so closely with people that we can take *everything* on board, possibly without realising it. In Santa Cruz, one year, I picked up all sorts of things from a guy I was working with - including his insomnia (and I am a professional sleeper). It was a very weird experience, and it took me several days to realise what I was doing; and then I could let it go.

The point about modelling is that, if we take on someone else's physiology, and somebody else's beliefs system, we can also take on their diseases - unless we realise what we're doing. Robert Dilts's mother, Patricia, was written off by the doctors who pronounced that they could do no more for her: she had a recurrence of her breast cancer, and she was going to die; so that was that.

It was at this point (in 1982) that Robert took over her treatment; he discovered that Patricia's mother and her elder sister had been her role models; and they had both died of breast cancer. Patricia believed that she had no right to recover, because how could she be in any way better than them - they were her role models? Fortunately, Robert has a sister, and so he was able to ask Patricia what would happen to *her* daughter, if *her* role model died of breast cancer. The mother instinct proved stronger than the modelling instinct, and Patricia realised that, if her daughter were to remain healthy, it was up to *her* to break the pattern. So she broke it and, for another fourteen years, became a warm, healthy, glowing model to us all. Her story is listed in the Bibliography, and you will find Robert's version in his '*Beliefs*'.

There is a myth (or what Robert aptly calls 'a thought virus') going round that baldness too is inherited and that therefore, as with all so-called 'inherited' diseases, nothing can be done. My husband works with Natural Hair Products, and they have masses of people regrowing their hair - many of whom had bald fathers or grandfathers.

Stress

Stress manifests itself in all sorts of shapes and guises from headaches and back-aches, to more serious things - if the owner has not paid attention to the first lot of messages.

Stress symptoms are simply communications from our selves to us; and, once again, we need to think about the positive intentions. Maybe we are not taking enough time for ourselves; maybe a symptom started as a wake-up call for us to step into action in time to meet our deadline, and we didn't pay attention to the meaning of the communication; maybe we are just driving ourselves too hard; maybe we feel that we are not in control of our lives; maybe we are not having enough fun - only your unconscious mind can tell you what it wants for you.

The once-bald David Clark-Wilson of Natural Hair Products expresses things better than I can: 'Taking an aspirin every time we have a headache is the same as ripping out the car's oil pressure gauge when the warning light comes on'. The headache, like the little red light, is a communication that we need to pay attention to.

Some people, on the other hand may not consciously have symptoms - they just feel pressurised, unhappy, depressed, gloomy, or something; and so, as you would expect, the question we ask here is: '*How do you know?*' How do they know they feel pressurised?

You may get a blank stare, when you ask this question; in which case you can explain - gently - that there are only five ways of knowing anything: we see it, we hear it, we feel it, we taste it and/or we smell it (think how some people tap their noses when they are suspicious of something). If someone - determined to go one better than you - asks triumphantly: 'What about intuition? The sixth sense?', you can continue - equally gently - that, once again this has got to come through one of the five senses; otherwise, how else can you possibly know? If you felt like it, you could add that the original Latin verb *tuere* meant 'to look upon': intuition is often an internal picture, which flashes past so fast that we may not be aware of it at a conscious level - although we may say things like: 'I knew in a flash'.

If we listen to the language of stress and depression, we can get valuable clues to work with:

- 'it has all built up.'

  *Q.*What has all built up?

  *Q.*How do you know it has all built up?

- 'everything has got on top of me'

  *Q.*How do you know that everything has got on top of you?

  A.'I feel trapped'

  *Q.*What do you feel trapped by? or

  Whereabouts in your body do you feel trapped?

And, if we watch at the same time, people will show us where it is all happening: they may move their hands around in the area where they are seeing (consciously or unconsciously) what they 'cannot face'; or indicate with a hand which ear the information is coming into, or where they are experiencing the feeling that they have got a problem.

As always, the trick is to repeat their own words and phrases back to them, rather than our interpretation of their words; this serves two purposes: (1) the person feels that we understand what they are experiencing - that we have joined them in their model of the world; (2) *their* description of what is going on inside them is the only valid one, in other words: how could I possibly tell you what is going on inside you? I am not there. For example, if you told me that everything looked 'rosy', and I said 'so everything looks bright' (which is what that might mean to me), this might not be the same thing at all: your 'rosiness' might be soft and warm and subtle, and you might find the idea of 'brightness' far too garish for what you were experiencing.

Jenny

Jenny came to see me, two years after her first visit. Last time it had been impending GCSE exams; this time, it was 'A' levels. She was (a) in a complete panic, because she had not got time to do all her work, (b) refusing to do any work anyway and (c) driving herself and her family mad with her apparent irrationality.

Jenny is extremely intelligent and, if this were just a question of rationality, she would have sorted out the problem, long since, for herself. So, how did she know she was in a panic? Well, she wasn't really sure..... (moving her hands around, in front of her eyes - not consciously aware of what was going on). Whatever she was seeing in her mind's eye was clearly too close for comfort, so I suggested she move it away to the opposite wall, where she could give herself enough space to see what it was all about; and there was this mass of stuff that needed to be done. There was an awful lot of it but, now that it was further away, she could look at it calmly, and divide it up into bite-size pieces.

So what was her outcome for taking these 'A' levels? To get to university and be independent. Jenny adores her family, but feels that everything is done for her at home, and that it is now time to create a life for herself. At this point, she went back to the mass on the wall, and described how and why she had chosen her 'A' level subjects, and how she wanted all her work to be personal to her, rather than copied out of textbooks.

And the positive intention for refusing to do any work? Like me, Jenny is a polarity responder: the moment anyone *tells* her what to do, she does the exact opposite. And so - even if she *had* just been thinking about doing some work - if her mother suggested it was time to do it, she would immediately go off the idea. It was simply about taking charge of her own life, and her own brain, and not letting anyone else interfere.

As we talked, she would keep glancing at the mass on the wall; and, the more we talked, the more she realised that, in fact, there really wasn't that much to be done, that she had plenty of time and that she was really going to enjoy doing it her way.

John

John was another polarity responder. He was under severe stress, and having serious health problems; all his family were saying: 'Go and see Diana', so he didn't. My hallucination was that he was trying to kill himself off; but, as he refused to consult me, there was not a lot I could do about it.

And then, one day, he telephoned and made an appointment. He arrived, gaunt and haggard, and weighing about half his original weight - and I knew he was dying. 'Oh, well', I thought to myself, 'at least now his survival instinct has overridden the self-destruct program. At last, now, we can do something'.

I chose to work standing up, so that I could keep John moving about because (a) if I kept his body moving, that would keep his brain from getting stuck, and (b) we could keep the thinking about the problem separated into its relevant places - rather than swirling around, in a muddled mass.

He told me that he could not '*see any way out*'; so I asked some more questions and discovered that, in his mind's eye, he was in a black box. I asked him to show me what shape it was, and his hands delineated a coffin.

John is inclined to be very left-brained and to think in small details, so I needed to use this to my advantage to forestall any possible argument: he would probably consider the idea of a positive intention as far too wishy-washy, so I told him, firmly, that he had invented this black box, and put himself in it, and asked him what stopped him from stepping out of it again.

There was the briefest of pauses, while I hallucinated that he was thinking that he couldn't, because the lid was nailed down; and then he realised that - logically - if he had invented the whole thing himself, the answer had to be 'nothing'.

So he took my hand, stepped out into the daylight, and has been going from strength to strength, ever since.

Stephen

An independent soul, who thought he ought to be able to sort his problems out for himself, finally consented to come and see me after his second suicide attempt: it was the horror and humiliation of finding himself a 'specimen' to be studied and cross-questioned in front of an auditorium full of students - when still in shock at finding himself alive - which made him realise that he needed to make some changes.

He described his situation as 'stuck'. And how did he know? He talked about the days when he had been '*running* a business' - when life was good, and fun and exciting. So what was he experiencing now? He felt as if he was '*walking* through treacle'. To be suddenly reduced from 'running' to walking through treacle, was pretty dramatic - no wonder he hated it. And, when he discovered that the positive intention of the treacle was simply to make him *slow down* and take stock of his new career, life became more interesting, and worth living again.

Viruses, the Immune System and Identity

If we equate the immune system with identity, in our logical levels, then we can become aware of how the immune system's job is to repel boarders: to keep us safe from pirates who might take over the ship and sail her under another flag.

Or we could think of viruses and bacteria as squatters; and the best way to keep squatters out is to be in ourselves. I very rarely get colds, but one day I woke up with squatters at every orifice, trying to get in; and so, just to see what would happen, I conjured up a state of total joy - through every cell of my body, and I could almost hear them saying: 'There's no point wasting time on this one: there's somebody at home'. And away they went.

There's the story about the man who was dying of cancer. There was nothing more the doctors could do for him, so he discharged himself from hospital, booked into an hotel, and hired videos of all his favourite comedy movies - because he had decided that he was, at least, going to laugh himself to death. And he laughed so much that he recovered.

Laughter, like joy, engages every cell of our bodies. We are at home: engaged, aligned and committed to ourselves. When did you last *allow yourself to laugh all the way down?*

*****

As a problem cannot be solved at its own level, we need to 'chunk up' to a higher level; in other words, if we are talking about a behaviour - at the 'what' level - it is much simpler to chunk up to the 'why', the 'who' or the 'who else' level. The presupposition of positive intentions goes straight to 'why', and we can generally work with that. However, in Patricia Dilts's case, when Robert discovered, at the 'why' level, that his mother believed that she must model her role models to the end, he realised that the problem was one of beliefs and identity. So he went straight up to the 'who else?' level, so that Patricia could discover for herself what would happen to the people who had taken her as a role model.

As you will have discovered, the name of any disease is not particularly relevant - unless it carries with it beliefs about 'incurability'; what we need to think about is the person in question, and how they have organised things inside themselves. Each of us is unique; each of us does our own thing in our own way; and each of us does the best we can with the resources that we have available to us at the time.

Creating Your Own Box of Delights

We are coming to the end of the beginning of this voyage of rediscovery of your self; and now might be a good time to ask yourself what has changed in your thinking? And what changes in your life have these changes in your thinking made? For example:

- How are you getting on with X - now that you know that his/her behaviour has a positive intention?
- How much interest are you finding in exploring other people's maps of the world?
- How many resources have you rediscovered for yourself?
- What is life like, with all these resources now available to you?
- How much simpler does life become when you are clear about what you want?
- What surprising changes are you noticing in the ways that you now react to what might once have seemed to be difficult situations?
- What happens to your relationships with other people, when you act as if every person you meet *really* matters to you?

and, more importantly:

- What changes have you made in the language you use to address your self?
- Now that you are treating your self with more respect, how has your relationship with one another changed?
- What else have you noticed?
- What other changes would you like to make?

For people who love DIY, NLP is a series of tools with which to make changes. If you are one of these, what kind of toolbox would be the best for you to carry around in your imagination - to house your collection? What is it made of? What colour is it? What shape is it? How many layers has it got?

For people like me, who only wield a screwdriver as a last resort - when we can't find anyone else to do it for us - the thought of 'tools' might not seem so exciting. It is up to you to decide what you wish to call all the stuff you have learned, and are continuing to learn - as you make use of what you have already discovered. You may think of it as toys to play with, or as treasures to enjoy and pass on to your descendants.............. or as something completely different.

Whatever you decide, you can create the equivalent of a toolbox to house them: it may be a golden treasure chest; or a velvet-lined jewel case; or an Aladdin's cave; or something completely different.

Everything and anything is available to you. Enjoy your self!

The Persian Rug

Once upon a time, in a land so far away that you would have to go all the way round the world to find it again, there lived a simple, happy, hard-working family who loved life and who loved each other very dearly.

One day they were discussing how to spend their hard-earned savings, and they decided that the one thing they needed to make their happiness complete was a hand-woven rug: something that would be beautiful to look at, that would feel good under their tired feet, and would soothe their tired eyes when they came in out of the blazing sun - a thing of beauty that would not only last them throughout their lives, but also bring joy to generations to come.

Delighted with this decision, they made their way to the Holy City where the first thing they did was to visit the designer whose work they liked best, and tell him exactly what they wanted: the rug was to represent the Tree of Life, and it was to be unique - specially designed for them. The designer asked a lot of questions so as to be sure they understood each other; and, as he listened to their answers, he became aware that this was to be the most beautiful and original rug he had ever designed.

It was to be woven from the finest wool - shorn from the chests and shoulders of lambs raised in the high mountains - and inlaid with silk. The Tree of Life would be a perfectly proportioned creation standing firmly on the ground, set beside a stream in a flowering forest full of birds and animals; the trunk rising gracefully and strongly towards the heavens and opening up into leafy, flowering branches, with the green of the leaves symbolising the constancy of ever-returning spring. And all this would be balanced and framed within its borders, so you could look deep into the design and lose yourself in its beauty, symmetry, harmony and balance.

Some time later, when the designer had worked everything out, down to the last knot, the family joined him for a visit to the dye master - a man with generations of carefully guarded secrets of his art - and they spent many hours wandering among shanks of seemingly endless bewitching, subtle and jewel-like colours of hand-spun wools and silks: comparing, contrasting, choosing, until everything was exactly to everybody's liking.

Now work on the rug could commence. They took the designer's pattern and the materials to the weavers and left them in their capable hands, knowing that they would have a long time to wait, and that the wait would be worth it.

The next visit the family paid was for the first shearing. The first few inches of the rug had been woven and the pile was about four inches long. Because this was such an important rug, the Master Shearer himself gave it his personal attention: using a special pair of scissors, he cut the pile down to about two inches and, suddenly, the beautiful pattern could be seen.

The weaving progressed and, as everybody knows, only Allah can make things perfectly, so the Deliberate Mistake was woven carefully into the rug so that He would not be offended.

The Knot Master himself did the most intricate of the knots, so that everything would be exactly as the designer and the family had dreamed - and better. Time went by and eventually the knotting was finished and the Master Shearer washed the rug by hand. Then he shaved it, to give it a smooth finish and ironed it to help it to lie flat.

The exquisite work of art was borne proudly to its new home, where the more they looked at it, the more they loved it. In the main border, sheep - the treasures of the region - stood among flowers and munched on fresh green leaves. Every plant, by the stream where the deer played, was different; every flower on the Tree of Life was different; every bunch of leaves was different; every bird was different. But what gave the rug the most distinction was the thin line of turquoise (a colour which can only be reproduced in the Holy City) which protected the trunk and branches of the Tree of Life - even where it had been pruned to encourage strong growth.

The children spent many happy hours searching for the Deliberate Mistake. They found it eventually: a tiny silken petal in one of the flowers was woven in a different colour.

The rug held pride of place and spent many years giving pleasure and delight to all who appreciated beautiful things, until one day a terrible thing happened. A visitor, wearing stiletto heels, walked on it. The rubber had come off one of her heels and, with the tremendous pressure put upon it, the

metal heel went straight through the trunk of the Tree of Life breaking the warp and weft threads. The rug was rushed back to the weavers, before any more damage could occur. It was carefully mended and looked as good as new.

However, all was not as well as it looked; something was wrong: the rug seemed to have lost its inner glow. Only those who knew and loved it realised that there was a difference - they examined it over and over again but could not find anything wrong. The repair had been done beautifully, but although an outsider could not find it, the family were aware of it - maybe only because they knew it was there.

They worried and talked about it endlessly: the Master Weaver was, by this time, a very old man; perhaps he had not even seen the rug; perhaps the repair had been done by a young, inexperienced weaver; perhaps (horror of horrors!) the wool used for the repair had been coloured with an aniline dye which had unbalanced the fine colours of the rest of the rug, and would also fade to a different colour. Carpet weaving was one of the oldest of crafts; every knot carried the wisdom of the ages. Perhaps the original knots were rejecting the new ones. The family went on searching for possible reasons for the change in their beloved rug.

Eventually, in desperation, they went to see the Master Weaver. Old though he was, he had not lost any of his sparkle. He had two distinguished visitors with him: two other famous Master Weavers. He was delighted to see our friends and even more delighted to see the rug, which he laid out proudly for his two colleagues to see while he sent for the Knot Master.

'Now tell me, distinguished friends', he said, when the Knot Master had arrived, 'what we did about the damage.'

'Genius, pure genius', they said, nodding their heads in awe, 'you had to make the Deliberate Mistake, so you used that to weave in some purple - the colour of magic spells and self-identity - and that has highlighted the whole of the strength of the trunk, and draws the attention deep into the being of the rug.'

'But', added the older of the visitors, 'this is a comparatively young rug; perhaps it was not aware of the high degree of magic involved. Every knot remembered the shock of the accident, and perhaps they were all afraid to find out what had been done in the repair work.'

As he was speaking, a change seemed to take place in the rug. The Master Weaver held up a hand for silence as they all saw, and felt deep within them, that a massive series of minor adjustments and rebalancing was taking place in the whole design. And, as they watched an inner light and warmth seemed to develop from inside the rug, which spread outwards all around it. The watchers each drew in a deep breath as the changes took place.

'Changes like this can take time', the Master Weaver said quietly, 'we shall allow them all the time they need.' And they watched and waited patiently, experiencing changes deep within themselves as they saw their beloved rug slowly and carefully restoring itself to its former glory.

'Take it home and love it', said the Master Weaver, 'and keep the knowledge you have acquired today deep within your hearts. It is there for you to use whenever you need it.'

Bibliography

Andreas, Steve & Connirae: *Change Your Mind - and Keep the Change*, Real People Press, USA, 1987

Andreas, Steve & Connirae: *The Heart of the Mind*, Real People Press, USA, 1989

Bandler, Richard & Grinder John: *The Structure of Magic I*, Science & Behaviour Books, USA, 1975

Bandler, Richard & Grinder, John: *Frogs into Princes*, Real People Press, USA, 1979

Bandler, Richard; Grinder, John & Satir, Virginia: *Changing with Families*, Science Behaviour Books, USA, 1976

Bandler, Richard: *Using your Brain - for a Change*, Real People Press, USA, 1985
Magic in Action, Meta Publications, USA, 1992
Time for a Change, Meta Publications, USA, 1993
*The Adventures of Anybody, Meta Publications, USA, 1993

*Bach, Richard: *A Gift of Wings*, Pan Books, 1976
Illusions, Pan Books, 1977
Jonathan Livingston Seagull, Pan Books, 1972
A Bridge Across Forever, Pan Books, 1985
One, Pan Books, 1988

Barlow, Wilfred: *The Alexander Principle*, Arrow Books, 1973

Bateson, Gregory: *Steps to an Ecology of Mind*, Jason Aronson Inc, USA, 1972
Mind and Nature, Bantam Books, 1988

Beaver, Diana: *Lazy Learning: Making the Most of the Brains You were Born With*, Element Books, 1994

Benjamin, Harry: *Better Sight without Glasses*, Thorsons, 1929

Berne, Eric: *Games People Play*, Penguin Books, 1964

Bertherat, Thérèse: *The Body has its Reasons*, Cedar Books, 1977

Bly, Robert: *Iron John: A Book about Men*, Vintage Books, USA, 1992

Brown, J A C: *The Social Psychology of Industry*, Penguin Business Library, 1954

Bryant, Andrew: *The Baldness Cure, Vermillion, 1994*

Burley-Allen, Madelyn: *Listening - the Forgotten Skill*, John Wiley, USA, 1982

Capra, Fritjof: *The Tao of Physics*, Flamingo, 1976
    Turning Point, Bantam Books, 1983

Cameron-Bandler, Leslie & Lebeau, Michael: *The Emotional Hostage*, Real
    People Press, USA, 1986

Carlzon, Jan: *Moments of Truth: New Strategies for Today's Customer-Driven
    Economy*, Harper & Row, 1989

Castaneda, Carlos: *The Teachings of Don Juan*, Penguin Books, 1970
    Tales of Power, Penguin Books, 1976
    The Eagle's Gift, Penguin Books, 1982
    The Second Ring of Power, Penguin Books, 1979

Charvet, Sheila Rose: *Words that Change Minds: Mastering the Language of
    Influence*, Anglo American Book Company, 1995

Chopra, Deepak: *Quantum Healing*, Bantam Books, 1989
    Creating Affluence, New World Library, USA, 1993

DeLozier, Judith & Grinder, John: *Turtles all the Way Down*, Grinder DeLozier
    Associates, USA, 1987

Dethlefsen Thorwald & Dahlke Rüdiger MD: *The Healing Power of Illness*,
    Element Books, 1993

Dilts, Robert: *Albert Einstein: Neuro-Linguistic Analysis of a Genius*, Dynamic
    Learning Center, PO Box 1112, Ben Lomond, CA 95005, USA, 1990
    Wolfgang Amadeus Mozart: Songs from the Spirit,(as above), 1992
    Skills for the Future (as above), 1993
    Changing Belief Systems with NLP, (as above), 1990
    Effective Presentation Skills, (as above), 1994
    Strategies of Genius, Vol I, (as above), 1994
    Strategies of Genius, Vol II, (as above), 1994
    Cognitive Patterns of Jesus of Nazareth, (as above), 1992
    Walt Disney: The Dreamer, the Realist and the Critic (as above), 1990
    Moshe Feldenkrais: NLP of the Body (as above), 1990
    The Parable of the Porpoise: A New Paradigm for Management (as
    above), 1990

Dilts, Robert B, Epstein Todd, and Dilts Robert W: *Tools for Dreamers*, Meta
    Publications (USA), 1991

Dilts, Patricia: *Pathway to Wholeness*, (DLC as above), 1992

Dilts, R, Hallbom T & Smith S: Beliefs: *Pathways to Health and Well-Being*,
    Metamorphous Press, USA, 1990

Edwards, Betty: *Drawing on the Right side of the Brain*, Fontana Books, 1979
    Drawing on the Artist within, Fontana Books, 1986

Eicher, James: *Making the Message Clear: Communicating for Business*, Grinder,
    DeLozier Assoc (USA), 1987

Feldenkrais, Moshe: *Awareness through Movement*, Penguin Books, 1980

Fisher, Roger & Ury, William: *Getting to Yes*, Hutchinson Business, 1981

Fritz, Robert: *The Path of Least Resistance*, Stillpoint, USA, 1984

Gallwey, Timothy W: *The Inner Game of Tennis*, Pan Books, 1975
    The Inner Game of Golf, Pan Books, 1981

Gallwey, Timothy W & Kriegel Robert: *The Inner Game of Skiing*, Pan Books,
    1977

Gilligan, Stephen G: *Therapeutic Trances*, Brunner/Mazel, New York, 1987

Goldberg, Herb: *The New Male*, Signet, 1980
    What Men Really Want, Signet, 1991

Goldratt, Elyahu M & Cox, Jeff: *The Goal: Excellence in Manufacturing*, North
    River Press Inc, USA, 1984

Gonzalez, Luis Jorge: *Jesus the Leader*, Editorial Font, Mexico, 1995
    Pleasure in Problem Solving, Editorial Font, Mexico, 1995
    Love, Health and Longevity, Editorial Font, Mexico, 1995
    Enjoy your Inner Artist, Editorial Font, Mexico, 1995

Gray, John: *Men are from Mars, Women are from Venus*, Thorsons, 1993

Green, Barry with Gallwey, Timothy W: *The Inner Game of Music*, Pan Books,
    1986

Greenwood, Michael & Nunn, Peter: *Paradox & Healing*, Paradox, Canada, 1992

Grinder, John & Bandler, Richard: *Trance-formations*, Real People Press, USA,
    1981

Hall, Michael: *The Spirit of NLP: The Process, Meaning and Criteria for Mastering
    NLP*, Anglo American Book Company, 1996

Hay, Louise L: *You Can Heal Your Life*, Eden Grove Editions, 1988

Jacobson, Sid: *Solution States: A Course in Solving Problems in Business With The
    Power of NLP*, Anglo American Book Company, 1996

Karbo, Joe: *The Lazy Man's Way to Riches*, Success Classics, 1986

Kingston, Karen: *Creating Sacred Space* with Feng Shui, Piatkus

Laborde, Genie, Z: *Fine Tune Your Brain*, Syntony, USA, 1988
Influencing with Integrity: *Management Skills for Communication and Negotiation*, Anglo American Book Company, 1997

Lakoff, Georg & Johnson, Mark: *Metaphors we Live By*, University of Chicago Press, USA, 1980

*Lynn, Jonathan & Jay, Anthony: *Yes Prime Minister*, BBC Publications, 1986

McMaster, Michael & Grinder, John: *Precision: A New Approach to Communication, Precision Models*, USA, 1980

Moore, Robert & Gilette, Douglas: *King, Warrior, Magician, Lover*, Harper, San Francisco, 1990

Morris, Desmond: *Manwatching*, Triad Panther, 1978

*Paulus, Trina: *Hope for the Flowers*, Paulist Press, USA, 1972

Richardson, Jerry: *The Magic of Rapport: How You Can Gain Personal Power in Any Situation*, Meta Publications, USA, 1987

Roberts, Monty: *The Man Who Listens to Horses*, Hutchinson, 1996

Rogers, Carl: *A Way of Being*, Houghton Mifflin Company, USA, 1980

Rogers, Carl: *Dialogues*, Constable, 1990

Rossi, Ernest Lawrence: *The Psychobiology of Mind-Body Healing*, Norton, 1988

Russell, Peter: *The Brain Book*, Routledge, 1979

*Saint-Exupery, Antoine de: *Le Petit Prince*, Gallimard, France, 1946

Sams, Jamie & Carson, David: *Medicine Cards*, Bear & Co, Santa Fe, New Mexico, 1988

*Satir, Virginia: *Self Esteem*, Celestial Arts, USA, 1975

*Satir, Virginia: *Meditations & Inspirations*, Celestial Arts, USA, 1985

Schwab, Joanna et al: *The Satir Approach to Communication*, Science and Behaviour Books, USA, 1989

Senge, Peter: *The Fifth Discipline: The Art and Practice of the Learning Organisation*, Doubleday, 1990

Seymour John & O'Connor Joseph: *An Introduction to Neuro Linguistic Programming*, Thorsons, 1993

Suzuki, Shinichi: *Nurtured by Love*, Ability Development, USA, 1983

Thich Nhat Hanh: *The Sun My Heart*, Parallax Press, USA, 1988

Whitmore, John: *Superdriver*, RAC, 1988

Zarro, Richard A and Blum, Peter: *The Phone Book: Breakthrough Neurolinguistic Skills for Profit and Enlightenment*, Metamorphous Press, USA, 1989

Zukov, Gary: *The Dancing Wu Li Masters*, Flamingo, 1982

* These are not textbooks, they are just to expand your thinking

A large number of these are available by mail order from Anglo American Books (see useful addresses).

Some Useful Addresses

The Anglo-American Book Company (Contacts: Martin and Glenys Roberts) (an excellent selection of mail-order NLP and related books)
Crown Buildings
Bancyfelin
Carmarthen SA33 5ND
Tel: 01267 211880. Fax: 01267 211882

The Association for Neuro-Linguistic Programming (Contact: Sue Gazey)
48 Corser Street
Stourbridge
West Midlands DY8 2DQ
Tel: 01384 443935. Fax: 01384 443931

Diana Beaver
C/o The Useful Book Company
P O Box 48
Cirencester
Gloucestershire GL7 5YE
Tel/fax: 01285 850155

McKenna Breen Ltd (Richard Bandler in England)
P O Box 10778
London N6 5FQ
Tel: 0181 340 8089. Fax: 0181 348 0629

The NLP University (Robert Dilts & Judith DeLozier)
(Contact: Teresa Epstein)
The Dynamic Learning Center
P O Box 1112
Ben Lomond
California 95005, USA
Tel: (408) 336 3457. Fax: (408) 336 5854

The First Institute (Richard Bandler, US) (Contact: Brahm von Huene)
238 Bush Street
San Francisco
California 94004, USA
Tel: (415) 882 4657

Index

Notes

Notes

Notes

Notes

Notes

Notes

Notes

Notes

Notes

Notes

Notes

Notes

Notes

Notes